Memories with Recipes

Memories *with* Recipes

An Autobiographical Cook Book

Ruth VanDyke

To order additional copies of this book, contact:
Xlibris
1-888-795-4274
www.Xlibris.com
Orders@Xlibris.com
764301

Dedication

To my soul mate, my children,
grandchildren, nephews, and nieces,
and all my wonderful friends,
I leave you with a legacy
I hope will never end.

My love and thanks to all of you,
the good and the bad, you saw me through.
May the memories of the smiles and laughter
live in your hearts forever after.

Acknowledgments

There are so many people I have to thank for this book: My beautiful granddaughter, Michelle, who first planted the seed. My agent, best friend, and husband Larry who spent many hours nourishing the seed and keeping it growing. My children who all survived my cooking for so many years with no complaints. All the wonderful friends who have crossed my path and without whom I would never have had so many food stories or recipes. My writing coach and mentor, Carol Purroy MA for her encouragement and guidance on this project. My friend and confidante Pam Durio who has been right next to me for the whole venture editing recipes for many hours.

Chapter 1

The bells of St. Mary's Church in Butte, Montana, were chiming the Angelus, as they did at seven o'clock every morning, when I made my entrance into this world. It was April 1940. My mother was also born and reared in Butte, "the richest hill on Earth." Her mother, Mary Therese Keating, was born in Leadville, Colorado, on March 14, 1880. When Mary was ten years of age, her elder brother Jerry took her to Butte when their mother died. Her mother's sister, Annie, who had six children of her own, raised her. Joseph Young, whose family had migrated from Canada, settled in Butte to make his fortune in the copper mines. Joseph and Mary married and had two little boys and a baby on the way when, on Saturday, October 23, 1909, Joseph was killed in a mining accident at the Little Minah mine, just one month before my mother was born. One of the so-called copper kings (the three men who controlled the mining industry in Butte at that time), F. Augustus Heinze, bought my grandmother a house where she raised her children. Every morning she would walk to the west side of town to clean the houses of the elite who lived in mansions. She would make just enough money each day to buy food for dinner and the next day's breakfast.

My first recollection of being aware of my love for food comes from fond memories of the smell of my paternal grandpa Keane's bakery. Joseph Keane was born in 1877 in East Meath, Meath County, Ireland. His family migrated to the United States in 1884. Joseph was one of fifteen children who grew up in Hell's Kitchen in New York City, where his eldest brother, Pat, worked as a cook. Grandpa and some of his brothers worked in a bakery, and he became the president of the first bakers union in New York. He was eventually run out of (or, as he liked to tell it, "politely asked to leave") the state because of union and political uprisings. His elder brother, Tom, moved to Connecticut to work in a bakery. One of my favorite stories about Tom is of the time when he and some of his coworkers lost their bakery jobs. The bakers would get the bread into the oven at night and then would have lunch and take a nap. When the bread was finished baking, the owner's pet monkey would wake them. Well, on one particular night in 1890, they woke up to the smell of burning bread. When Tom returned to New York City and was questioned as to why he lost his job, his answer was simply "The monkey died."

My father was one of seven John Francis Keanes born in New York City on December 5, 1903. There were three more children born to Joseph and Julia in New York—Joseph Jr., Victor, and Agnes Ruth. Grandpa moved his young family west to Montana and opened his first bakery in Butte in a basement near the corner of Park and Main Streets next to the old Rialto Theater. In 1923, the new Royal Bakery opened at 107 East Park Street. My father and my uncle Joe were both bakers, and my brother also worked at the bakery in his younger years. My very first job was at my grandpa's Bake-Rite bakery when I was in high school. Grandpa used to tease me about eating up all the profit. Oh, those vanilla wafers. I have yet to taste a cookie quite as delectable. I have not attempted to cut the recipe down to make just a couple of dozen, but I keep promising myself that I will someday.

I didn't realize it growing up, but my mother was not a very good cook. We were always fed well—fried potatoes, fried steak, fried pork chops, fried chicken, and fried eggs. Her recipe for meat loaf was one pound of ground beef, salt, pepper, and a loaf pan. We had salad with our dinner meal almost every day; it consisted of lettuce, tomato, and Miracle Whip. On special occasions, when bananas were available (which, in the 1940s in Montana, was not all that often), we were treated to banana salad: sliced bananas and Miracle Whip, topped with walnuts if we happened to have them. Friday was macaroni-and-cheese day, unless, by chance, someone brought us fresh trout. Mother's macaroni and cheese (which I loved as a child and still sometimes long for) was made with Velveeta cheese and—no, not Miracle Whip—ketchup. She always managed to produce awesome traditional holiday dinners. Her gravy was one of the things in which she excelled, the other being the wonderful candies that she made at Christmastime. I have never been able to duplicate my mother's divinity.

***

From Mother's Kitchen
Divinity

3 cups of sugar   ⅔ cup of light corn syrup
⅔ cup of hot water

Boil to hardball stage (250–266°F).

2 egg whites
A pinch of salt

Beat egg whites until stiff peaks form. Pour syrup over egg whites slowly while beating. Drop by tablespoon on wax paper.

Caramels

2 cups of sugar   ½ teaspoon of salt
2 cups of white corn syrup   ½ cup of butter
2 cups of heavy cream (or canned evaporated milk)
1 teaspoon of vanilla

Stirring occasionally, boil the sugar, salt, and corn syrup to 245°F (very thick syrup). Add butter and then milk gradually so that the mixture does not stop boiling at any time. Stir constantly and cook rapidly to the firm ball stage. This mixture is very thick and sticks easily at the last minute. Add vanilla and pour into greased pan. Cool thoroughly before cutting. Cut with heavy sharp knife using saw-like motion.

Penuche

2 cups of brown sugar
1 cup of canned evaporated milk
¼ teaspoon of salt
½ cup of chopped pecans

1 cup of white sugar
2 tablespoons of light corn syrup
1 teaspoon of vanilla

Stir together brown sugar, white sugar, milk, corn syrup, and salt. Cook to softball stage (234–240°F). Remove from heat and cool without stirring until the bottom of the pan is lukewarm. Add vanilla and beat until creamy. Stir in pecans. Pour into buttered eight-by-eight-inch square pan. Cool and cut into squares.

Pecan Pralines

1 ¾ cups of granulated sugar
⅛ teaspoon of salt
1 cup of water

1 tablespoon of butter
¼ teaspoon of maple flavoring
1 ½ cups of pecans

Melt half a cup of sugar in skillet over low heat, stirring constantly until the sugar forms a pale yellow syrup. Remove from heat and let stand for five minutes. Add salt, water, and remaining sugar. Stir carefully until caramel is dissolved. Add butter and cook to softball stage (236°F), stirring constantly. Remove from heat. Add flavoring and pecans and stir until mixture becomes creamy. Drop by teaspoons onto wax paper. Makes about one pound.

Two-Tone Fudge

Combine two cups of firmly packed brown sugar, one cup of granulated sugar, one cup of evaporated milk, and half a cup of butter in a saucepan. Bring to a full boil over moderate heat, stirring constantly. Boil for ten minutes, stirring occasionally. Remove from heat. Add one jar of marshmallow cream (five-to-ten-ounce jar) and one teaspoon of vanilla, and stir until mixture is smooth. To two cups of hot mixture, add one six-ounce package (one cup) of butterscotch-flavored morsels and half a cup of coarsely chopped walnuts. Stir until the morsels are melted and the mixture is smooth. Pour evenly into a greased nine-inch square pan. To the remaining hot mixture, add one six-ounce package (one cup) of semisweet chocolate morsels and half a cup of coarsely chopped walnuts. Stir until morsels are melted and mixture is smooth. Pour evenly over butterscotch mixture in pan. Chill until firm. Makes about two and a half pounds.

***

While we are on the subject of fudge, I want to share a recipe that my mother sent to me in the early 1960s with the notation "Had to send this. It is so like you." She was referring to the fact that I was notorious for saying things backward. This recipe spoof was published in the local newspaper in Butte on April Fool's Day from a long out-of-print cookbook.

Mrs. Spooner's Fut Nudge

2 buttlespoons of taibler	2 cups of shanulated grugar
3 cuppers quart of crinn	Theme or boff of the tottle
2 chalks of squairkolet	2 spaible tunes of sorn keerup
1 nup of kelled shuts	A vittle lanilla

Shook the kugar, the chilk, the mawkolet, and the sorn keerup until the mawkolet chelts. Stoil withoub burring to 234 degees of greet. Then dairfully crop a little of the mott hixture into a wawt of cold cupper. If little bawft sawls form in the cuttum of the bopp, the dudge is fun. Remove the hann from the peat, bad the utter, let canned until stool, and fladd the aivoring. Speat with a boon until gick and thooey, mopp in the druts, empty into battered pun, and squark in mairs. You may marsh addmellows if you have a particularly teet swooth. Serves a gruzen doan-ups or two bean-aged toys.

If you would like to unscramble it, it may make a good fudge. I've never tried it, so good luck!

***

One of the things my mother liked to make when she entertained her bridge club at our house or for guests was a specialty of hers that I have never, ever, come across anywhere else. We loved these gooey sandwiches as kids, and my daughter makes them on occasion, although I don't think anyone but she and I really like them. Mother called them sloppy joes. They are nothing like the hamburger sloppy joes that we are familiar with today. The name on the recipe card that I got from her years ago reads the following:

Stuffed Finger Rolls

1 ½ dozen hot-dog buns
1 pound of American cheese (Velveeta)
1 can of pimentos
3 hard-boiled eggs, chopped
½ cup of black olives, chopped
½ cup of vegetable oil
1 can of tomato soup
½ teaspoon of salt
1 tablespoon of Worcestershire sauce

Fill rolls, wrap in wax paper (or foil), and heat for twenty minutes in a 325-degree oven. My mother always said they tasted better if heated in wax paper.

***

Another of her favorites when she entertained was a Jell-O-cheese salad, which I have made often over the years.

Jell-O-Cheese Salad

1 3 oz. package of lemon Jell-O
1 3 oz. package of lime Jell-O
3 cups of boiling water
¼ cup of lemon juice
¾ cup of crushed pineapple
1 cup of heavy cream
1 package of cream cheese
½ cup of chopped celery
½ cup of chopped walnuts

Dissolve Jell-O in boiling water. Add lemon juice and then chill slightly until soupy. Whip cream and combine with cream cheese. Add remaining ingredients and chill.

***

Some of my fondest memories of growing up in Butte are the times we spent at Uncle Keeny and Aunt Betty's house out on "the flat." Living up on the hill in Butte, everything south of Front Street was referred to as "the flat." My aunt Betty was short and rotund and was the most humorous person I knew in my young life. Thinking of her now brings to mind the original Betty Boop. Oh, how she made me giggle whenever I was with her. I could be in another room and burst out in laughter just hearing her laugh.

Aunt Betty's house was on Harrison Avenue, right next door to the fire station. It had what seemed to me the largest front porch in the world. The family would gather there on the Fourth of July to watch what I also thought was the biggest parade anywhere. My uncle had a parrot who could wolf-whistle just like a human. Perched on his stand on the porch, he would whistle at the girls passing by, getting my uncle in trouble more than once.

They also had an English bulldog, and whenever we were there, they would warn my mother, "Watch the baby [me]. We don't want the dog to bite her." One day, while the family was visiting in the living room and the dog was napping under the dining-room table, there came a bloodcurdling yelp from the dining room. They quickly ran to find me under the table, chewing on the dog's ear. I guess I had decided that I would bite him before he could bite me.

I was only five years old when the Japanese surrender was announced on August 14, 1945. Celebrations erupted across the United States, and Butte was always up for a celebration of any kind. Cars were driving up and down Harrison Avenue, blowing horns, waving flags, throwing firecrackers and confetti, and screaming. I was so frightened. I remember huddling down in the corner of the porch and crying. I did not understand that this was the moment that Americans had hoped for since the attack on Pearl Harbor in December 1941.

My uncle lifted me in the air, chanting, "The war is over, the war is over!"

***

Aunt Betty loved to cook, and we all loved her cooking. I am sorry that the only recipes I have of hers are the Christmas cakes that she made for us every year.

Christmas White Cake

2 cups of sugar
¾ cup pf butter
7 eggs, beaten one at a time
2 heaping cups of flour, not sifted before measured
1 teaspoon of baking powder
1 teaspoon of vanilla
1 teaspoon lemon flavoring
1 pound of white raisins
1 cup of walnuts
½ pound of pecans
2 large slices of fresh pineapple
½ pound of candied cherries

Mix all ingredients. Bake at 275 degrees for half an hour, and then turn up to three hundred degrees and bake for one more hour. Makes two loaves.

Brazil Nut Bread

Preheat oven to 300°F.

¾ cup of sifted all-purpose flour	1 teaspoon of vanilla
½ teaspoon of salt	3 cups of shelled Brazil nuts
¾ cup of granulated sugar	1 pound of pitted dates
1 teaspoon of baking powder	1 cup of well-drained Maraschino cherries
3 eggs	

Grease and then line with waxed paper a nine-by-five-by-three-inch loaf pan. Sift together flour, salt, sugar, and baking powder. In large bowl, place nuts, dates, cherries. Mix into flour mixture by hand until the nuts and fruits are well coated. Beat eggs until foamy and add vanilla. Add to flour mixture. Spread evenly in pan. Bake for one hour and forty-five minutes until done. Cool in pan on rack for fifteen minutes. Remove from pan and peel off paper. Cool on rack. Wrap in aluminum foil and then store in refrigerator.

***

Butte became a city in 1876, and by 1885, the population had grown to over twenty thousand. Many of these people were Irish and Cornish immigrants who made their way west to work in the copper mines. By 1918, the population is said to have reached close to a hundred thousand, making it the largest city west of the Mississippi. It was claimed to be the most prosperous town in the entire United States. There were as many as fifty nationalities represented. Each ethnic group brought their traditional customs and foods, most of which carry over even today.

The Cornish pasty can be traced back as far as the thirteenth century in Cornwall, England. Mining was a thriving industry in Cornwall, and the pasty was a mainstay for the miner's lunch bucket. Legend has it that the thick crimped edge was for the miners to hold onto while eating the meat pie. Their hands would be covered with arsenic from the mine, so they would just discard the handle when they finished eating the pie. Ask any miner about the "knockers" who inhabited the mines, and they will assure you that these leftover crusts kept the ghosts content.

The miners referred to the pasty as a "letter from 'ome." Every household seemed to have their favorite recipe for this delicious meat-and-potato pie. The Cornish insist that the meat must be sliced, but the American version is usually with sirloin steak, diced, according to some bakers, "the size of the third joint of a Cornish woman's little finger." Then there are those of us who prefer ground meat. My mother's crust recipe is the best I have ever eaten, and I have never found it in any cookbook. I use this crust recipe also for my pies. It is easy to roll out and freezes well for later use.

***

Cornish Pasties

Pastry:

4 ½ cups of flour   1 teaspoon of baking powder
1 teaspoon of salt   2 cups of shortening or lard

Cut shortening into flour, baking powder, and salt.

Beat one egg with one tablespoon of white vinegar and one cup of cold water. Mix into flour mixture. Dough will seem too moist, but knead until it holds together. Roll out rounds to size of pasty desired.

Filling:

2 pounds of meat (use sirloin tip, skirting, flank steak, or ground meat)
5 or 6 medium potatoes
2 yellow onions, chopped
Salt and pepper

Mix together, using about a third of a pound meat for each pasty. The meat may be diced or sliced. Potatoes can also be either diced or sliced. When I use ground meat, I grate the potatoes. Mix ingredients together or layer meat, potatoes, and onions onto pastry rounds. Fold pastry over meat mixture and crimp, dampening the dough to seal. Brush tops lightly with egg wash (egg yolk and water) or milk. Bake at four hundred degrees Fahrenheit for fifteen minutes and then at 350 degrees for one hour.

The traditional pasty (the "oggie") was made with rutabaga added.

***

For wonderful hors d'oeuvres or finger snacks, I make the following:

Mini Pasties

Roll out piecrust dough and cut in three-inch circles. Mix one pound of ground sirloin steak with one package of dry onion soup mix, salt, and pepper. Scoop one tablespoon of meat mixture onto dough. Fold over and crimp edges. Bake at 350 degrees for thirty to forty minutes.

***

I don't know when or how it became traditional to serve coleslaw with pasties, but for as long as I can remember and wherever pasties were served, coleslaw was the accompaniment. I have tasted a lot of soggy or watery cabbage slaw, some too sour, some too sweet, but the following recipe is, without any doubt, the most creamy and delicious ever. It is best prepared a day or two before serving.

Mike's Coleslaw

1 two-pound head of green cabbage
2 carrots
1 small green pepper (optional)
3 tablespoons of vinegar
⅓ cup of sugar
1 ½ cups of mayonnaise

Shred cabbage and carrots. Finely mince green pepper. Combine. Mix vinegar, sugar, and mayo in blender or vigorously by hand. Put half of the cabbage mixture into a two-quart casserole or bowl. Pour half of the dressing over it. Add remaining cabbage and dressing. Cover and refrigerate. Stir well before serving.

In 1979, my friend Nancy Foley McLaughlin opened a pasty shop in Butte after much encouraging from her family and friends. Nancy and I were born on the same day in the same hospital and went through high school together. One cannot pass through Butte without stopping for one of her famous pasties. There is a restaurant in Las Vegas that serves as many as thirteen varieties of pasties plus fifteen different premium pasties and several dessert pasties, everything from Cajun chicken, salmon, and Reuben and Guinness stew to apple caramel or peanut butter and jelly.

The Italian immigrants who settled in Butte lived on the east side of town in an area known as Meaderville. They brought with them their old-country traditions as well as their wonderful cooking talents and recipes. There were boarding houses in Meaderville in the early mining days that fed and housed hundreds of miners. When I was growing up, Meaderville was the place to go if you were looking for a night out for dinner, dancing, and gambling. The restaurants all served multicourse dinners, beginning with plates of antipasto, raviolis, and spaghetti and wonderful Italian breads. Even though it wasn't of Italian descent, Mrs. Sylvain's sweet-potato salad was always a side dish. By the time the main course was served, we were usually too full to eat it. Luigi had his one-man band playing nightly at his club, and you could stop in at the 45 Club or the Arrow for a hot game of poker. During the days of the Prohibition, Meaderville was referred to as Little Monte Carlo. Weddings, graduation parties, and almost any special occasion could be held at the Rocky Mountain Café.

***

This sweet-potato salad originated from the Roadhouse at the 5 Mile Casino, which, in the 1940s, became Lydia's. You can still enjoy the Italian-style meals served at Lydia's, which is now in town. I made this salad as a traditional Easter dish for my family for many years but gave up on it when no one would eat it but me. It is delicious. I don't know if Durkee's dressing is readily available today, but it is a must for this salad.

Sweet-Potato Salad

1 pound of sweet potatoes, boiled with skins, cooled, peeled, and mashed
3 or 4 stalks of chopped celery
2 scallions (green onions), chopped
4 hard-boiled eggs, chopped
Dash of salt and pepper to taste

Mash potatoes, mix in remaining ingredients, and add enough mayonnaise and Durkee's dressing to moisten. Cover and refrigerate four to six hours before serving.

***

Ask anyone in Butte, and they will tell you that there is just one original Pork Chop John's. Located on West Mercury Street, John's is noted for its scrumptious deep-fried breaded pork-loin sandwich. The little shop is busy at any time of day or night. When I was in high school, after our "mixer" dances on Friday night, we would sit in front of John's and watch the clock for the midnight hour as most of us were Catholic and wouldn't eat meat on Friday. I am not sure how my brother came about getting this recipe, but it is supposedly the original.

***

John's Original Pork-Chop Sandwich

Loin pork, boned and fat trimmed off
White cornmeal

Slice pork into chops. Pound each chop thin with a meat pounder or the edge of a saucer. Pound in white cornmeal (not too much or it will make the meat doughy). Batter for two pounds of meat:

1 cup of flour

1 teaspoon of salt

⅔ cup of milk

2 eggs

½ teaspoon of white pepper

Add dry ingredients and milk alternately to beaten eggs. Dip meat in batter (let excess batter drip off). Fry in deep fat until brown. Place on paper towel to absorb grease. Serve on hamburger buns with sliced onion, dill pickle, and mustard.

***

I was given another recipe for pork-chop sandwiches, being told that it was John's original. I've tried them both and like them equally.

Pork-Chop Sandwich Number Two

Use thick-cut pork pieces or pork chops.

1 slightly beaten egg

½ cup of water

2 cups of flour

Dash of salt and pepper

1 teaspoon of melted butter or margarine

1 can (12 oz.) of evaporated milk

½ teaspoon of baking powder

White cornmeal

Mix all ingredients except cornmeal until smooth. Do not overbeat. Cut bone from pork chop and pound to flatten pork slightly. Dip each piece in batter and then roll in cornmeal. Cook in deep fat at 350 degrees until brown and well done. Place on hamburger buns with your own choice of relish.

***

I grew up on the east side of town in a housing project that was built in the 1940s in an area originally known as the Cabbage Patch. I have a dear friend who was raised in Centerville, a burg on the north hill of Butte, who calls me the original Cabbage Patch Kid. Silver Bow Homes was low-cost housing, so it was occupied mainly by older folks and poor people. No one ever told me that we were poor, however. I grew up contentedly, not wanting for anything. We didn't always have the best, but we were clean, well fed, and properly dressed at all times. I was a happy-go-lucky child, surrounded by music and laughter.

I was not able to start first grade at the beginning of the school year because I had rheumatic fever. I was fearful and anxious when the day came that I had to attend school. Sacred Heart School was one of nine parochial grade schools in Butte in the 1940s. It was built in the late 1890s or early 1900s on East Park Street. It smelled of mold and stale urine. A narrow spiral stairway led to the musky basement where the bathrooms and auditorium were located. By third grade, I had myself and most of the other kids convinced that the basement was haunted, and I spent eight long years trying to avoid descending those stairs alone.

The Reverend Edmond Taylor was the pastor of Sacred Heart Parish. He was a gargantuan ruddy-faced Irishman whose voice was powerful enough to scare off the devil himself. His brogue was so heavy that I wasn't quite sure what he was saying to me, and that made me very nervous. My mother laughed when I came home wide-eyed and shaky, telling her about this scary man. She dug out her 1923 eighth-grade graduation picture, and there he was, a young handsome Irish priest, Father Taylor. When she—a shy, quiet girl—was in the fourth grade, Father Taylor hit her on the back of the head with a heavy hardbound catechism book because she couldn't answer a religion question. Obviously, no one had warned Father Taylor about her feisty, four-foot, eleven-inch, red-headed mother. My grandmother's visit to the rectory was the object of gossip throughout the parish. Father Taylor would cross the street to avoid her from that day forward.

In my eighth-grade graduation picture, as in my mother's, there he is, "the man," Father Taylor, who, during my most impressionable years, taught me not only the importance of education but also how to savor every amusing, laughable, priceless moment of our lives and to never, ever, give into anything contrary to our beliefs. He embedded in me the fear of God and the love of mankind.

The east side of town was also home to the shady, non-glamorous red-light district, where the girls of the night entertained the miners as well as the upright white-collared business men. East Mercury Street was off-limits for us to even walk past. The infamous Venus Alley had individual cribs with private entrances on each side. The Dumas brothel operated until 1982. It is now a frequently visited museum, offering tourists an inside look of how the oldest profession flourished.

So many memories of growing up in Butte flood my mind. Every Thursday was "Children's Day" at the Columbia Gardens. The city buses were free, and we would pack our lunch in paper bags and head to the most wonderful amusement park and beautiful flower gardens for a day of fun. I think of it now as the precursor to Disneyland. This magical place, at the foot of the Rocky Mountains, was a gift to the people of Butte from W. A. Clark, another one of the copper kings in 1899. Even now, I can close my eyes and remember going through the turnstile at the gate and the smell of the popcorn as we walked up the boardwalk, past the concessions and games, toward the old rickety wooden roller coaster and the flying biplanes. The greatest thrill was riding the ornate carousel. We all seemed to have our favorite horse, and as the music accelerated, our laughter blended in with the tempo. Up the hill to the playground and the popular "cowboy swings" and the dollhouse and "Mrs. Meany," the playground monitor, whom we all loved to hate. Happy, carefree days, never to be forgotten.

On November 12, 1973, Columbia Gardens, my sixty-eight acres of heaven, burned to the ground.

Anyone who grew up in Butte could ever forget Chinatown or "China Alley," as we called it as kids. When the Chinese miners came to work in the copper mines, they brought with them their customs, traditions, and food. By 1900, there were seven noodle parlors flourishing in town. Some people say that a trip to Butte is not complete without a visit to the Peking Noodle Parlor. The old Mai Wah building now houses exhibits of the opium dens and the Asian history in Butte. Just north of where we lived in Silver Bow Homes, there were two large brick buildings; one was the Chinese laundry, and adjacent to it was the workers' living quarters. I vividly recall my fear when I had to walk past there as a child. My heart would pound, my palms would sweat, and I would break into a run. What was I afraid of? I have never been able to answer that question.

I remember the excitement of being treated to banana splits at Gamer's on Park Street. It opened in 1905 and is still in business, a busy spot for breakfast. One critic said, "Be sure to sit at the counter to get a good history lesson on Butte from one of the old-timers." The locals are all very proud of their heritage and delighted to share it with anyone willing to listen.

Another memorable eatery was the Red Rooster out on Harrison Avenue. The sign read, "Come as you are." Back then, we would never have dreamed of showing up in pajama bottoms and slippers. The cold sandwiches that they served were piled so high with turkey, ham, or beef that you could hardly get your mouth around them.

My mom worked at a little hole-in-the-wall restaurant, the Sip and Bite, on West Broadway, in her younger years. She liked to tell about the older gentleman with no teeth who would come in every day and order "thoup and thumpin' thoft."

The iconic M&M Cigar Store on North Main Street opened in 1890. The beat poet Jack Kerouac described it in a 1970 article for *Esquire* magazine as the "ideal bar," with characters ranging from "old prospectors, gamblers, whores, miners, Indians, and cowboys to tobacco-chewing businessmen." The miners worked in shifts and could always have a hot meal or grab a quick beer at this popular twenty-four-hour "joint," as my dad called it. It was a sad day in April 2003 when the doors closed for the first time in 113 years. It is now reopened, serving breakfast, lunch, and dinner at very affordable prices. Good food, good fun, and the rallying point every year for Butte's notorious Saint Patrick's Day parade. According to a 2010 census, Butte is the most Irish city in America, with a 23.6 percent Irish population, compared to Boston's 19.8 percent.

Speaking of parades, Butte's Fourth of July celebration is second to none. I smile remembering Tony Kononika leading the parade every year. He was the junkman of Butte, and his shop on East Park Street had anything and everything that you couldn't find anywhere else. He was an eccentric old fellow who knew everybody in town. The basement of his shop, where most people were not allowed to go, was lined with old slot machines and sewing machines, wringer washing machines and machines too many to mention. I don't know when he died or whatever became of his wonderful treasures, but I do remember that he lead the parade in a vehicle when he could no longer walk.

The Fourth of July celebration was an all-day party for all ages, beginning with the grandiose parade. Marching bands and elegantly decorated floats, horses and fire trucks, clowns and drill teams paraded all the way through town, from uptown all the way out to the "flat." The day ended with the giant fireworks display on Big Butte, the landmark hill on the west side of town, home to the big M, which lights up the skies every night, representing the Montana School of Mines, one of the most prestigious mining schools in the country. A bronze statue of Marcus Daly, the third of the copper kings who discovered that there was copper in the Anaconda Mine and went on to build the huge Anaconda Copper Mining empire, stands proudly overlooking the School of Mines. It was said of Marcus Daly, "In life, he never turned his arse on the mines of Butte or the miners who dug them" (Matty Kiely in Copper Camp).

Just before my seventh birthday in April 1947, my mother married the kindest, most loving, soft-spoken, funniest, humble man I have ever known. He wanted to get married on April Fool's Day, but Mother wouldn't hear of it. George had never been married and didn't have children. He would tease my mother, telling her that he only married her for her kids. I couldn't have hoped for a better dad. He adored my mother. When he was young and she worked at the local movie theater, he would go there just to see her, not the movie. She didn't even know he existed at that time.

My pa, as we called him, was an underground copper miner. His father was said to have walked from Hungary to Germany before migrating to America in 1905. His mother, Bella, died in 1922 at thirty-four years of age. His elder sister, Ella, was just fourteen, and she quit school to take care of her younger brothers. George was ten years old, Johnny eight, Dan six, and the baby, Billy, was three. Ella devoted her entire life to raising these boys. She was a fabulous cook. She loved baking bread and taught many people the art of making *povitica*. She and her brother John owned and operated one of Butte's west-side neighborhood grocery stores for twenty years. I can still visualize the glass dishes in the display case that held the penny candy. I loved the holidays at my aunt Ella's. It was exciting for me, having this new extended family.

The word *povitica* means "to roll" in Slovenian. The dough should be rolled thin enough to read the paper through it, I was told by a baker. There are several published recipes for this bread but none to compare with that of my aunt Ella. She taught my mother how to make it, and Mother, in her later years, showed me how, but I have only made it once. My niece Ronda makes it almost every Christmas and still uses the tablecloth that my mother used to roll out the dough. My cousin Kay, who has become an expert at the art of making this delectable bread, gave me Ella's original recipe.

***

Ella's Famous Walnut Povitica

Filling:

> 2 pounds of walnuts, ground fine (4 cups of walnuts will equal
> 1 pound)
> 1 cup of sugar

Mix together and add enough water to make a thick batter. Bring to bubbling stage on stove top or microwave. Then cool and add two eggs and one cup of sugar, beaten together with one teaspoon of vanilla.

Dough:

> 1 tablespoon of dry yeast in ½ cup of warm water in mixing bowl

Sift together six and a half cups flour and two teaspoons salt. Scald two cups of milk, and then add one stick of butter. Cool and add one teaspoon of vanilla. Add two eggs and half a cup of sugar to the yeast. Then combine all ingredients. Mix lightly, and let rise in a greased bowl. Top with a little melted butter. The dough will be very sticky. Let rise one hour, maybe fifteen minutes longer. Punch down dough and let set for fifteen minutes. Then divide in half.

Place a tablecloth on the table and sprinkle with flour. Put half of the dough in the center, roll out into a circle as far as you can, spread the top with melted butter, and then stretch with buttered hands until the table is covered with a thin layer. (Note: Kay uses a forty-two-inch round table, and it is covered.) If you have a large table, you can stretch all the dough at once.

Trim thick edges off and top with the cooled filling. Spread filling and then top with more melted butter and sprinkle with a little sugar. Pick up the edge of the tablecloth, and the filled dough will roll into a jelly-roll type. Then coil the roll like a snake into a roasting pan that you have lined with parchment paper or silicate. Let the *povitica* rise a second time, about one to one and a quarter hours. Bake at four hundred degrees for half an hour and then at 325 degrees for about one and a quarter hours. Test with probe to 190-degree temperature. Half of this recipe will fill a nine-by-thirteen inch pan.

Note from Kay: When you are making this, raise the temperature of the room and the humidity. She uses a humidifier and a small heater under the table before stretching the dough.

Ella's Cheese Povitica

6 cups of flour

⅞ cups of warm water

2 teaspoons of salt

½ stick of butter (melted)

Mix in food processor. The dough will be sticky. Let sit for fifteen minutes. The room needs to be warm and humid. Divide dough in half and stretch each half on floured tablecloth. Top with cottage cheese (a little less than one quart). Roll as a jelly-roll, coil into baking pan. Use silicate or parchment paper on the bottom of the pan and grease well so that it won't stick. Bake at 350 degrees for one hour and fifteen minutes. This can also be used with sliced apples instead of cottage cheese to make apple strudel.

Ella's Chocolate Sour Cream Cookies

2 cups of flour

½ teaspoon of baking soda

½ cup of butter

1 cup of sour cream

½ cup of chocolate chips

½ cup of cocoa

½ teaspoon of salt

1 cup of sugar

1 teaspoon of vanilla

1 egg

Mix flour, cocoa, soda, and salt. Beat butter and sugar until fluffy. Add egg, sour cream, and vanilla. Beat well. Add flour mixture and chocolate chips. Drop by teaspoons onto greased cookie sheet. Bake at 375 degrees for ten minutes.

***

In 1953, we moved into a brand-new house on the upper west side (the "right" side of the tracks). My mother was thrilled with her first new home, but I refused to change schools. There were no school buses back then, so I had to take the city bus across town every day to school. I didn't mind though. It seemed much easier to me than having to make new friends. It turned out to be a very advantageous move as in 1955, we watched a big part of the east side of town disappear when the Berkeley Pit, the new open-pit copper mine, began to swallow up neighborhoods, including Meaderville, Dublin Gulch, and all the McQueen area. Copper prices were the highest they had been since 1918, and the Berkeley Pit was producing about three hundred thousand tons of material daily and had extended to within four blocks of the center of town. The beautiful Spanish mission-style Catholic church, Sacred Heart, was demolished, as were the grade school and many east-side businesses. It is said that between 1955 and 1982, "the richest hill on Earth" produced enough copper to pave a four-lane highway four inches thick from Butte to thirty miles past Salt Lake City (Pit Watch — Berkeley Pit News and Information).

My high-school days were busy and too quickly gone. My love of dance took as much time as my schoolwork. My only regret is that I didn't realize the importance of my education at that time. Learning came very easy to me, and I always managed to maintain good grades without much effort. I was a band majorette for two years and danced with an Irish dance troupe that entertained during the month of March every year. Making costumes for the dance recitals, talent shows, ice skating, and Friday-night dances at the old Sons of St. George's Hall in Centerville made for a busy, active lifestyle.

My longing for travel and my gypsy blood gave way to any rational plan for the future when I met Patrick O'Neill. He was home on leave from the navy, and when he met me, his buddy Joe told him, "There is no way she would even glance your way. She's one of those hard-to-get type of girls."

When Pat offered me and my friend Maureen a ride home from the drag races, I told her, "I wouldn't be seen dead with him."

Well, fate has a way of playing itself out, and after a two-month long-distance-mail romance, he returned, unannounced, to Butte to whisk me off my feet, marry me, and take me 1,600 miles away from home to Oklahoma. My dad's heart was broken. He had huge hopes for my future. We were married at the Immaculate Conception Church in August 1957 with our childhood friends as witnesses. As we drove out of town the next day, my eyes welled up with tears as I saw through the rearview mirror my papa's beautiful Highlands, the magnificent mountains surrounding the only home I had ever known, and the monumental Gallus frames lining the hills in every direction.

Butte will always be home to me, and now when I return, I am greeted by the magnificent statue of Our Lady of the Rockies, standing ninety feet atop the Continental Divide. The statue was constructed by volunteers using donated materials. It was a six-year project dedicated to women everywhere and can be seen lit for miles at night. My mom and dad watched from their back porch as the head section was placed atop the statue by the Nevada Air National Guard helicopter team on December 17, 1985. In 2007, the National Folk Festival was held in Butte, drawing thousands of people from all over the world.

A three-year-old boy questioned his dad, "Who is that up on the hill?"

His father explained that it was the Virgin Mary.

"Well, who is she?" the lad inquired.

"She is Jesus's mother," his dad replied.

The little boy's eyes lit up as he quipped, "I didn't know that Jesus was born in Butte."

Chapter 2

Leaving my home and starting a new chapter in life was exciting but, for a very young bride, a little bit scary. I had no idea what life would have in store for me. Our trip to Oklahoma was not exactly a honeymoon trip, as we were pressed for time. We stopped only once, in Jackson, Wyoming, to visit briefly with Pat's aunt Edna and uncle Slim. Slim was the deputy sheriff in Jackson Hole. He was a big John Wayne type of guy who won my heart when he sat beside the fire and read Robert Service poetry to me. If you are ever in Jackson Hole, you will see the large elk antler arches in the town square. Slim began collecting the shed antlers at an early age and designed and built these arches.

In 1958, while building a new ski lift, Slim was in a concrete bucket, working on installing the lines, and something went terribly wrong. The bucket was dropped several thousand feet down the mountain. I felt honored to have known him even for such a short time and think of him whenever I see an old John Wayne movie or pick up my well-worn poetry book.

Pat had arranged for us to move into base housing. We had a cute little furnished apartment, one set of sheets, one blanket, a coffee pot, and an iris-and-herringbone-depression glass sugar and creamer that my grandmother had taken off her kitchen table to give us as a wedding gift, nothing else. Pat had to check into his duty station the day after we arrived, so I had my first taste ever of being alone, no phone, and he took the car. I was afraid to even go for a walk and had no one to talk to. My mind wandered to my friends back home, getting ready to start back to school.

Oh my god, what have I done? This was the first of many "I want my mommy" moments. But everything was sunshine and roses again when Pat arrived home, held me in his arms, and promised that he would take care of me forever. Forever turned out to be sixteen years.

The day after arriving in Norman, we ventured out to buy what necessities we thought we needed. We needed everything, but on a petty officer's third-class wages, we knew that we had to budget carefully.

When I confessed that I didn't know how to cook, he assured me that it was no problem. "We can buy a can opener and a can of Dinty Moore Beef Stew."

We spent $31.31 on groceries. It was so many groceries that it filled up the back of the car. I still have the sales tape. We purchased a cheap set of aluminum pots and pans. They didn't have Teflon back then, and never having cooked, I was not aware that you had to use oil, bacon grease, or butter to fry an egg. Needless to say, our first breakfast was something right out of a slapstick movie.

"It's okay," he smiled as he scraped the burned scrambled eggs off the bottom of the pan.

We had enough money left over after our shopping spree to buy a little portable radio. Having music in our new home was very important to me.

After the egg incident, I was a little leery about trying my cooking skills (or lack thereof). One of the things I had brought with me was my 1953 edition of *Better Homes and Gardens New Cook Book*, which had been a requirement for my home-economics class. I studied that book as if it were a textbook for at least a month before I mustered up enough courage to try to make biscuits.

I wish I could recount for you the look on my husband's face when I took out of the oven what he later tagged my "silver dollar" biscuits. They had risen about a quarter inch, and if you dropped one on your foot, it could possibly break a toe. My children still laugh about my "silver dollar" biscuits. It took several years before I discovered a wonderful biscuit mix. Just add water, knead a bit, and voilà! Perfect biscuits every time. I do claim them as homemade. If I stir the batter and bake them in my oven, they are, without any doubt, homemade by me.

November rolled around, and by then, I was beginning to feel a little bit homesick, longing to be with my family for the holidays. I was thinking about my mom's turkey gravy, and in a moment of enlightenment, I decided that I could make a wonderful, memorable Thanksgiving dinner. We bought a little turkey and all the trimmings and carefully planned out the menu. I was so excited to embark on my first big cooking venture.

"Oh no, we don't have a roasting pan, and we sure as heck can't afford to buy one after all that we spent on the food," I lamented.

Pat, always the problem solver, smiled as he assured me, "That bird is small enough to cook in the large frying pan."

I stuffed the bird and was quite proud of myself for following the recipe to a T. The oven was heated, and I was right on schedule with the potatoes, yams, cauliflower, and fresh cranberry sauce. The aroma coming from the kitchen was divine, and I was feeling like a gourmet chef.

Time to take the bird out of the oven. No one ever told me—nor did I figure it out myself—that handles on frying pans are *not* oven proof. Being very cautious and using my new pot holders, I gingerly lifted the pan from the oven rack.

I heard behind me, "Be careful, and don't burn yourself."

In a split second, I was holding a pan handle. The pan was on the floor, and the bird was sliding down the slanted kitchen floor toward the hallway. I have no words to describe my devastation.

I was sitting on the kitchen floor, crying, while Pat was trying hard not to laugh and telling me, "It's okay. We can wash it off. It's edible."

Through my tears, as I looked at the greasy mess on the floor, I sobbed, "But there goes my gravy."

We made friends quickly with a young couple, John and Tommie, who lived in the same housing complex. They were from Texas, and as soon as we got acquainted, they began to tease me about my accent. *My* accent? I had never been around Southerners, so they sounded pretty strange to me.

"Why don't y'all spend Christmas with us and our families in Dallas?" John drawled.

"What a great idea! Thank you for inviting us," I squealed.

I was so excited to be going to Texas. When we arrived in Dallas, I was in awe of the skyscrapers. This was the first big city I had ever seen. John told me that a man fell from one of those buildings.

When I gasped in shock, he said, "Oh, the fall didn't kill him."

"Really?" I whispered in wide-eyed disbelief.

"Naw, it was the sudden landing."

John was quite the joker, a big tease, but so much fun to be around.

Tommie and I decided that we would make fudge for Christmas. She and I were in the kitchen at her mom's house; the guys were watching TV in the family room. I had never made fudge with marshmallow cream. Come to think of it, I had never made fudge at all. As I was carefully reading the recipe on the jar label, Tommie gave me the easy job of greasing the pan. I scooped up a big tablespoon of shortening just as John walked into the kitchen. He, thinking it was marshmallow cream, opened his mouth widely, and I could not resist cramming the spoon into his mouth.

His arms flailed wildly as he spat and screamed, "I'll get even with you, girl!"

This was my first Christmas away from home, and one of things that I learned was that cookies are love. We didn't have much to give monetarily, so I decided to make cookies for everyone. My first attempt at baking was from a recipe that one of my neighbors gave me for Mexican wedding cakes. Some people call them Russian tea cakes. I was tickled pink to see everyone so grateful for my meager gift. I have made this cookie every Christmas since 1957.

***

Mexican Wedding Cakes

1 cup of butter
2 ¼ cups of flour
1 teaspoon of vanilla

½ cup of confectioners' sugar
¼ teaspoon of salt
¾ cup of finely chopped pecans

Mix butter, sugar, and vanilla thoroughly. (The lady who gave me this recipe told me to mix and mix and mix.) Stir flour and salt together; blend in. Mix in nuts. Chill dough. Roll into one-inch balls. Place on ungreased baking sheet and bake in four-hundred-degree oven for ten to twelve minutes until set but not brown. While still warm, roll in confectioners' sugar. When cool, roll in sugar again. Makes about four dozen cookies.

***

We found a little house to rent in Downtown Norman. It was, in fact, a converted garage—living room, kitchen, bedroom, and bathroom all compacted into an area about the size of the living room in our previous apartment. I fell in love with the tiny kitchen and decided that it needed a bright yellow paint job and new seat covers on the two chrome chairs and frilly print curtains. The landlady, Ms. Wilson, a petite seventy-something typical Southern belle with a much-accentuated Southern accent, offered to give us a month's free rent for my kitchen renovation. My dad was appalled to hear that we were paying $85 a month to live in someone's garage when he was only getting $35 a month for his flats in Butte.

The day we moved in, Ms. Wilson told me to just help myself to the "okry" in the back garden. I had no idea what she was talking about. I smiled graciously and said thank you. A couple of days later, she came to the door with a colander full of something I had never seen or heard of before—fresh homegrown okra. I thanked her and put it in the fridge, hoping to find someone who could tell me what it was and what to do with it. It ended up in the trash a week or so later, and I prayed that she wouldn't ask me how I liked it or how I cooked it. I later learned to love fried okra.

Our first son was born on July 1, 1958. My mother came from Montana to be with me. Oklahoma summers are definitely not for the faint of heart or anyone who has never been in temperatures over eighty-five degrees, with humidity just about as high. I was concerned about her traveling that far on the train at her age. She was all of forty-nine! She carried a hand towel over her arm the entire time she was there to dab the constant beads of perspiration on her forehead.

Coming from the West, I had never been around tornadoes and didn't quite comprehend the danger.

When we were told to go to the shelter, I just scoffed and said, "I don't think that's necessary."

Oh boy, did I have a rude awakening when a thunderous blast wiped out several homes just across the street from us. It turned out to be one of the worst tornadoes to ever hit that section of Oklahoma. This was just my first encounter with the wrath of nature.

In the summer of 1959, Pat received orders for a new duty station, Roosevelt Roads, Puerto Rico. At about this same time, we found out that we would have a new addition to our family in December. I had to wait for housing to be available in Puerto Rico, so I planned to spend some time with my family in Butte. I was very relieved to be out of tornado country.

On August 17, shortly after we had retired for the night, I heard a deep rumble. It was stronger and louder than any thunder I had ever heard. Then the crib my son was in came flying across the room toward the hide-a-bed where I was sleeping, and the old wooden wagon-wheel chandelier swayed so hard that it hit the ceiling. My dad came running out of the bedroom. I had never seen him in his underwear before! He grabbed the crib and pulled it under the beams between the rooms. The shaking continued for what felt like an hour, but it was, in fact, only minutes.

This was the 7.3-magnitude earthquake that killed twenty-eight people camping at Hebgen Lake. The earth that crumbled from the mountain blocked the Madison River flow, which, after three weeks, created a lake more than 170 feet deep, five miles long, and a third of a mile wide. Today the lake is known as Quake Lake. There is a monument there to honor the people who lost their lives while camping that clear, still, starry night. There were several aftershocks the next day, and I couldn't help but ponder that this made the tornado seem much less frightening.

Within a month of experiencing this horrific earthquake, I left Montana to reunite with my husband in the home he had found for us in Puerto Rico. Traveling six months pregnant with a thirty-three-pound fourteen-month-old who refused to walk more than three feet on his own proved to be more of a challenge than I had anticipated.

Stepping off the plane at O'Hare Airport in Chicago was, without a doubt, the scariest moment of my life—that is, until we landed in San Juan and there was no one there to meet me. I didn't know where to go, and no one spoke English. When my husband finally found me and Patrick crying in the cafeteria, he was in near hysteria. He had been delayed at the base because of a typhoon that had hit the island of Vieques, just off the coast of Roosevelt Roads, where he was stationed. He had no way to contact me. Wow, I had just missed experiencing my third natural disaster in three months. A tornado in Oklahoma, an earthquake in Montana, and now a tropical typhoon—I was beginning to believe that Mother Nature was out to get me.

The new base housing was not yet completed, so we were assigned to temporary housing in the little village of Fajardo. Patrick, who was just learning to talk, quickly learned to speak Spanish.

"Hablo español, Momma," he would coax me.

It was such a delight to see this young toe-headed boy chitchatting with the old Puerto Rican men in the town square. They would talk and laugh, and I had no idea what they were saying.

The little native women would smile at me and rub my very pregnant tummy and offer me local food. This is how my love affair with mangoes came to be. We had a mango tree in our front yard, and I had avoided picking the strange fruit, which was as foreign to me as Ms. Wilson's "okry." Once I savored the sweet, juicy flesh hiding under the tough skin, I could not get enough of it. I was eating so much of this newfound scrumptious fruit that I just wasn't hungry for anything else. The obstetrician I was seeing became concerned that I wasn't gaining any weight. When he inquired as to my diet and I confessed to eating up to eight mangoes a day, he just smiled and assured me that it was okay.

Our second son, Don, was born in December 1959 at Rodriguez Army Hospital at the old El Morro Fort. There were no doors or windows at the fort at that time, but it was the only military hospital in the area. We had chosen the name Donald if the baby was a boy and Dawn Marie for a girl. I wanted to have my dad's name, George, for a middle name for a boy. My husband would not agree on it, so we had not made a final decision on a name. When the hospital requested me to fill out the birth certificate information, Pat was not there, so I had to decide what the baby's name would be.

When he arrived later that evening and inquired as to what I had given for a name, I jovially told him, "Well, we had agreed on Don, and since John is my favorite boy's name and with the baby being born at Rodriguez, I thought that Don Juan Rodriguez O'Neill would be quite fitting."

His jaw dropped, and a look of shock and disappointment came over his face.

I couldn't keep from laughing when I asked him, "Would Donald George [the name I had chosen] be more acceptable?"

"Oh yes," came his sigh of relief and half-assed grin.

Living in navy housing made it very easy to make new friends. Other young couples with small children and older grandparent-image folks were quick to welcome us into our new environment. The conversations usually turned to food and exchanging recipes or planning get-togethers. I had not, up to this point, been very creative with cooking or trying new dishes, so this became a challenge for me.

The first friends we made were a couple from North Carolina. Evelyn and Curtis were expecting their first child when we met them. She was the kind of a cook who could create a banquet from whatever she happened to find in the pantry. Evelyn made fried chicken that

that would put Colonel Sanders to shame. She had no recipe for it, just seasoned the chicken with salt and pepper and shook it in flour in a brown paper bag (a paper poke, as she called it) and then fried it to a golden brown in shortening. I have never, to this day, had fried chicken as good as hers. I have been trying for fifty years to replicate her "finger-lickin' good" chicken but haven't mastered it yet. Paula Deen's comes in at a close second. We tried it in Atlanta (along with fried okra) when we were there a few years ago.

***

The first cake I ever made was from a recipe given to me by Evelyn. This is still my "go-to" cake anytime I am hurried or unsure what to make for any event.

Lemon Jell-O Cake

1 package of yellow cake mix	1 package of lemon Jell-O
4 eggs	¾ cup of water
¾ cup of vegetable oil	1 teaspoon of lemon extract

Beat for four minutes at medium speed. Bake in tube or Bundt pan at 350 degrees for forty-five minutes.

Glaze for Lemon Jell-O Cake

| ½ cup of confectioners' sugar | 1 tablespoon of butter |
| Juice of ½ lemon | Grated rind of 1 lemon |

Mix and pour over cake while still warm.

***

Another cake she made, which I had never even heard of at the time, was a scrumptious carrot cake.

Carrot Cake

2 cups of sugar   1 ½ cups of salad oil
4 eggs   1 teaspoon of vanilla
2 ½ cups of self-rising flour

Mix sugar, oil, eggs, and vanilla together. Add flour gradually. Then add the following:

2 teaspoons of cinnamon   3 cups of grated carrots

Bake at 350 degrees for thirty minutes in three (eight-inch) greased and floured cake pans.

Filling for Carrot Cake

1 stick of butter (¼ pound), softened   1 pound of confectioners' sugar
1 teaspoon of vanilla   8 ounces of cream cheese, softened
1 cup of finely chopped walnuts

Mix all together and spread on cooled cake.

Christmas 1960 turned out to be one of my most memorable holidays ever and will always be my favorite food story. We had invited several neighbors to the house on Christmas Eve. Once we had the boys tucked into bed (with visions of sugarplums), we began to assemble their new swing set and wrap presents.

About 11:00 p.m., I decided that I wanted to go to the base chapel for midnight mass. "Who would like to go to midnight mass with me?"

No one replied or seemed interested. The liquor was flowing freely, and spirits were high.

"That's okay, I don't mind going alone," I said to no one listening as I walked out the door.

When I arrived home after mass, the party was still going strong. I was tired and knew that I had a big day approaching, so I excused myself. "Night, everyone."

I fell asleep quickly in spite of the music and laughter and slept soundly.

I awoke in the morning to the smell of coffee brewing and bacon frying. I jumped into my robe, and when I got to the kitchen, there was a tall handsome young man standing at my stove.

"Good mornin', ma'am." He smiled shyly. "Corporal Jennings at your service."

My husband had followed me to the kitchen, and he seemed thrilled to have his breakfast cooking and spoke with this guy as though he had known him all his life. I could only imagine at this point that it had been a good party the night before.

Over breakfast, Max Jennings let me know in his slow Southern drawl, "This is your day to enjoy with your children, ma'am. It will be my pleasure to prepare your Christmas dinner."

He proceeded to tell me that he was a cook at the marine barracks, and since he had no family here with him, he wanted to spend Christmas with us. Pat was smiling and nodding, so who was I to object?

As soon as Max cleaned up the breakfast dishes, he started preparing dinner. "I'll have to go back to the base to pick up a few things," he informed me, and he was gone for about an hour.

I had invited our neighbors to dinner, and I was feeling a little amiss about not doing the cooking. "There will be nine of us, including you, for dinner," I informed Max when he returned.

He was fine with that. He refused to even let me in the kitchen and announced, "Dinner will be at exactly 5:30 p.m."

Our guests arrived early and were all quite curious about my personal cook. I set the table, and we took our places. Max marched into the dining room, carrying a humongous domed platter (one of his reasons for going back to the base).

"We will say grace now," he announced, which was obviously a thorn in the sides of a couple of the guests.

With a strong amen, he flamboyantly lifted the dome, and there on the silver platter was a skimpy little game hen. When the laughter and applause subsided, he returned from the kitchen with a beautifully browned fifteen-pound turkey with all the trimmings. What a glorious, memorable meal. He did all the dishes and left my kitchen spotless, as if it had never been used.

He hugged the kids and, teary-eyed, very softly mumbled, "Thank you for a wonderful Christmas," and away he went.

"Wow," my husband remarked, still in awe of the phenomenal meal we had experienced. "Did you meet that guy at midnight mass?"

What? "No, he was here when I came home from church. I thought he was a guest at your party last night."

It turned out that neither one of us knew who he was or where he came from.

When my husband inquired at the marine base a couple of weeks later, planning to invite him to dinner, the officer in charge of the galley told him, "Oh, Max was transferred a few weeks ago." We never saw him again.

***

I think fondly of Max every Christmas and make his fresh cranberry salad every time I cook a turkey or game hens.

Max's Fresh Cranberry Salad

1 pound of fresh cranberries, crushed (I do them in the food processor or blender)
2 cups of sugar

Marinate berries in sugar overnight.

1 can (20 oz.) of crushed pineapple, drained
1 cup (maybe a little more) of miniature marshmallows
1 container (8 oz.) of Cool Whip

Mix ingredients, cover, and refrigerate.

***

Always having had a sweet tooth, and with the boys getting old enough to enjoy desserts, I became intrigued with easy dessert recipes. I made friends with a middle-aged woman whose children were already grown, and she found such pleasure in sharing her knowledge of "healthy treats," as she called them. So here are a few of Bernie Harris's favorite goodies.

Rice Pudding

⅓ cup of sugar
1 teaspoon of vanilla
2 well-beaten eggs
⅓ cup of seedless raisins

¼ teaspoon of salt
1 ½ cups of milk
2 cups of cooked rice

Combine all ingredients. Pour into lightly oiled one-and-one-quart baking dish. Sprinkle with nutmeg and cinnamon. Place in pan of water and bake in moderate oven (350 degrees) for about fifty minutes or until a knife inserted in the center comes out clean.

***

Bernie was of English descent, and English toffee was her favorite dessert. I haven't made it since the kids were little. They loved it.

English Toffee Dessert

1 cup of butter
2 cups of powdered sugar
3 beaten egg yolks

2 squares of melted baking chocolate
1 teaspoon of vanilla
1 cup of chopped nuts

Cream butter and add other ingredients. Fold in beaten egg yolks. Grease bottom of eight-by-eight-inch with butter. Add crushed vanilla wafers on bottom of pan. Spread mixture and add additional crushed wafers on top. Freeze. Cut in squares. Serve with a dash of whipped cream and top with a cherry.

Bavarian Cream

1 package (3 oz.) of any flavored Jell-O
¼ cup of sugar
1 cup of boiling water
¾ cup of cold water
1 envelope of Dream Whip

Dissolve Jell-O and sugar in boiling water. Add cold water. Chill until slightly thickened. Whip Dream Whip according to package directions. Blend one and a half cups into Jell-O. Pour into one-quart mold or six to eight individual molds. Chill until firm. Unmold and top with remaining Dream Whip.

***

Smarty Pie is the quickest dessert I have ever made. It was given to me by a goofy neighbor in Puerto Rico named Sally. She made this recipe up one evening when she was a little tipsy and craving something sweet. It is quick and topped with a little whipped cream or served warm with vanilla ice cream, it makes for a delightful dessert.

Smarty Pie

Melt a quarter pound of butter or margarine in a nine-by-nine-inch baking dish.

Mix lightly the following:

1 cup of sugar	¾ cup of flour
¾ cup of milk	1 teaspoon of baking powder
Pinch of salt	

Pour into pan with butter. Do not stir. Pour in one large can of fruit with heavy syrup. Bake for forty minutes at 350 degrees.

***

Another delectable sweet treat of Bernie's was her orange cookies. She made them often for my kids, and when she left for a new duty station, she gave me the recipe and told me to never let my boys forget her. So many, many years ago. These were one of their favorite cookies.

Bernie's Real Orange Cookies

2 ½ cups of sifted flour	2 eggs
½ teaspoon of salt	1 tablespoon of grated orange rind
½ teaspoon of baking soda	½ cup of orange juice
½ cup of shortening	½ cup of walnuts or coconut
1 cup of sugar	

Sift flour, salt, and baking soda together. Cream shortening, sugar, and eggs. Mix in flour alternately with orange juice and then mix in nuts or coconut. Drop by teaspoons two inches apart on greased cookie sheet. Bake at four hundred degrees ten to twelve minutes or until golden. Frost with orange butter icing: butter, powdered sugar, and orange juice. Sprinkle with coconut or chopped walnuts.

Whenever we had a get-together or potluck dinner, someone would always request Bernie's applesauce cake.

***

Applesauce Cake

½ cup of shortening
2 cups of sugar
1 large egg
1 ½ cups of applesauce
2 ½ cups of sifted flour
1 cup of walnuts, chopped

1 ½ teaspoons of baking soda
1 ½ teaspoons of salt
¾ teaspoon of cinnamon
½ teaspoon each of cloves and allspice
½ cup of water

Set oven for moderate—350 degrees. Cream shortening and sugar until fluffy. Beat in egg and then applesauce. Mix and sift flour, baking soda, salt, and spices. Stir into applesauce mixture alternately with water. Stir in walnuts. Bake forty-five to fifty minutes in oblong pan (nine by thirteen inches). Frost as desired.

***

In June 1962, Pat was accepted into submarine school in New London, Connecticut. We had the opportunity to take a ship back to the States. Son Patrick celebrated his fourth birthday on board the ship with a party that was given for him and another little boy. They had a huge birthday cake and gave him a Candy Land game, which occupied most of our time for the rest of the sailing.

It was very early in the morning when the ship pulled into New York Harbor. Through the foggy mist, I got my first glimpse of the Statue of Liberty. The ferry boats were tooting a "welcome home" to us, and all the passengers began to cheer. A feeling of pride that I had never known came over me as tears of joy rolled down my cheeks. We were about to embark on yet another exciting new adventure.

We moved into navy housing in Groton, Connecticut, near the submarine base. Our new neighbors were all young couples attending school there. Everyone got together for a welcome party, and I met a delightful lady, Rene, who taught me to make the most delicious baked spareribs I had ever tasted. She called them baked spareribs "aloha," a recipe that she had brought from her homeland in the South Pacific. As a side dish, she served Hawaiian skillet beans. I have a food allergy to dry beans, so I wasn't able to eat them, but I have served them many times over the years, and they are always a hit.

***

Baked Spareribs "Aloha"

3 pounds of lean sparerib
Salt and pepper
½ cup of finely diced onion
¼ cup of diced green pepper
2 8 oz. cans of tomato sauce
1 tablespoon of Worcestershire sauce
⅓ cup of vinegar
1 20 oz. can of pineapple tidbits (use syrup)
¼ cup of brown sugar
½ teaspoon of dry mustard

Cut after every third rib about halfway through the strip. Sprinkle with salt and pepper.

Place in shallow roasting pan. Bake in moderate oven (350 degrees) for one and a quarter hours. Drain off all excess fat. While ribs are roasting, mix remaining ingredients and let stand to blend flavor. Pour over ribs after baking. Bake forty-five to fifty minutes longer, basting frequently to coat the ribs with the flavorful sauce.

Hawaiian Skillet Beans

8 slices of bacon	2 cans (one pound each) of pork and beans
5 slices of pineapple	2 tablespoons of brown sugar

Cook bacon in skillet until crisp. Drain on paper towel and crumble coarsely. Pour off all but two tablespoons of drippings. Sauté pineapple until lightly browned. Remove from heat. Combine beans, brown sugar, and crumbled bacon in skillet. Heat thoroughly. Top with pineapple slices. Heat until bubbly.

***

Another side dish that was inexpensive to make and convenient for our group get-togethers was a veggie pilaf that was great served with chicken or fish.

Vegetable Pilaf

In two tablespoons of butter in a skillet, sauté half a cup of chopped onion until tender but not brown. Toss in one cup of raw regular or processed white rice. Arrange in a greased one-and-a-half-quart casserole. Pour on one can of condensed chicken broth, undiluted. Cover and bake in 350-degree oven for thirty to thirty-five minutes or until all the liquid has been absorbed and the rice feels tender between your fingers. Uncover at once. Meanwhile, in three tablespoons of melted butter in skillet, sauté one pound of mushrooms, sliced, for six to eight minutes. Also heat a one-pound can of green beans as label directs. Just before serving, toss rice with mushrooms and drained beans. Serve as side with chicken or fish.

***

One of the officer's wives at the submarine base in Groton gave me this recipe in 1962. It had supposedly been given to one of her relatives by Jacqueline Kennedy, who was, at that time, the first lady of our country.

Prune Cake

½ cup of shortening
½ teaspoon of soda
1 cup of sugar
½ teaspoon of salt
2 whole eggs
½ teaspoon of cinnamon
1 ⅓ cups of flour
½ teaspoon of nutmeg
⅔ cup of chopped prunes
½ teaspoon of allspice
⅔ cup of sour milk (or buttermilk)
½ teaspoon of baking powder

Cream shortening. Add sugar and eggs and beat well. Mix dry ingredients and add alternately with sour milk to creamed mixture. Add chopped prunes. Bake in two eight-inch waxed-paper-lined cake pans for twenty-five minutes at 350 degrees.

Frosting for Prune Cake

2 tablespoons of butter
½ teaspoon of cinnamon
½ teaspoon of salt

2 tablespoons of prune juice
1 tablespoon of lemon juice
1 ½ cups of powdered sugar

Cream butter. Add prune and lemon juice, salt, and cinnamon. Beat in powdered sugar gradually.

***

Pat receive orders in 1963 to Norfolk, Virginia, for his first submarine duty. He had submitted a request for the first nuclear submarine, the *Nautalis*, or its sister ship, the *Thresher*. When his orders came through for an older Balao-class diesel-electric boat, the USS *Carp*, his disappointment couldn't be denied.

While he was on his first patrol on the *Carp* (or *Crap*, as he called it), I received the news that the *Thresher* had been lost at sea with all hands aboard during a deep-diving test about 220 miles east of Boston. A hundred and twenty-nine dedicated sailors, husbands, fathers, sons, and brothers would not be returning home. I sobbed uncontrollably as my friend Evelyn tried to comfort me. I was thankful that his request had been denied, but my heart was breaking for the families who lost their loved ones.

Raymond was born in August that year, and three months after his birth, I was hospitalized for gall bladder surgery. My mother flew from Montana to take care of the boys since their dad was on deployment. While I was in the hospital, my son Don, who was four years old at the time, told my mother that he wanted "floffers." She had no idea what he was talking about. When his elder brother Patrick told her that he wanted waffles, she laughed.

"Honey, I can't make you waffles. You have no waffle iron."

"My mommy makes them in the toaster" was his quick response.

She had never seen toaster waffles. Before she left to go back home, she bought me a waffle iron.

When Pat returned home after his three-month tour, we bought our first home, and our firstborn son started school. His first-grade teacher was the sister of one of my grade-school classmates. This was the first of many "small world" cases that we encountered over the years.

We lived just a couple of blocks from the Sears Service Department, and I took an evening job three nights a week so I could buy a dryer. Six years of hanging diapers was enough. Pat was on shore duty and was home from the base by 4:00 p.m. every day, so I would have dinner on the table at four-thirty, eat with my family, and leave him to do the dishes, spend the evening with the kids, and have them bathed and tucked in bed when I got home at nine o'clock. I did telephone solicitation, selling service contracts. I enjoyed my time being with adults and getting paid for it, and the kids were loving their time with Dad.

The lady who trained me for my new job was also a navy wife. When I asked her where she was from, she smiled and said, "Pennsylvania."

"Oh, where in Pennsylvania?" I inquired.

Her reply took me by surprise. "I don't like to tell people my hometown." She looked past me and seemed quite aloof.

I persisted, and she finally moved closer to me and whispered, "I'm from Intercourse, Pennsylvania."

One of the men in the room heard her and, trying to keep his composure, inquired, "Well, what do you say when people want to know where you live?"

She smiled and, not realizing the humor in her answer, quipped, "I just tell them, up the road apiece."

***

I loved my new kitchen and spent hours baking and cooking. I went on what I later called my "pie to die for" regime. Using my mother's crust recipe, I set out to make the perfect lemon meringue pie.

The Perfect Lemon Meringue Pie

1 ½ cups of sugar
⅓ cup of cornstarch
¼ teaspoon of salt
¼ cup of lemon juice

4 egg yolks, slightly beaten
2 tablespoons of butter
2 tablespoons of grated lemon peel

In a heavy two-quart saucepan, combine sugar, cornstarch, and salt. Gradually stir in one and a half cups of water. Over medium heat, bring to a boil, stirring constantly. Boil for one minute. Mixture will be thick and translucent. Remove from heat. Stir a little of the hot mixture into egg yolks in small bowl; mix well. Pour back into saucepan. Add the grated lemon peel. Stir constantly over medium heat until mixture boils again. Boil for one minute. Remove from heat. Add butter and stir until melted. Gradually stir in lemon juice. Fill nine-inch cooled pie shell.

Meringue:

Have egg whites at room temperature in medium bowl.

⅔ cup of egg whites (4 large eggs)
¼ teaspoon of salt
½ teaspoon of cream of tartar
⅔ cup of sugar

Preheat oven to 375°F. Beat egg whites until foamy. Add salt and cream of tartar. Beat just to blend well. Add sugar, one tablespoon at a time, beating well after each addition. Continue beating until meringue is shiny and stiff peaks form when beater is slowly raised—about five minutes. Spread meringue over cooled filling, sealing edge all the way around. Swirl meringue with back of spoon to make peaks. Bake twelve to fifteen minutes or until lightly browned. Cool on wire rack away from drafts until bottom of pie is at room temperature.

***

I was so impressed with the outcome of my first pie that I ate most of it myself! Although I have tried several other lemon meringue recipes, this is the best one I have found.

Being smugly pleased with my pie, I decided to make a chocolate cream pie from an old 1934 Hershey's cookbook. It is a simple recipe, using cocoa instead of the usual called-for baking chocolate.

This has, over the years, become my family's favorite pie. My son Patrick, from the first time I made it, requested it for his birthday every year in lieu of a birthday cake.

***

Cocoa Cream Pie

¼ cup of Hershey's cocoa
3 tablespoons of cornstarch
2 cups of milk
1 tablespoon of butter

¾ cup of granulated sugar
¼ teaspoon of salt
2 egg yolks
1 teaspoon of vanilla

Mix together cocoa, sugar, cornstarch, and salt in a saucepan. Gradually stir in milk, mixing well until smooth. Cook over medium heat until filling thickens, stirring constantly. Boil one minute and remove from heat. Slowly stir about half the chocolate mixture into slightly beaten egg yolks. Then blend into hot mixture in saucepan. Boil one minute more, stirring constantly. Remove from heat and blend in butter and vanilla. Pour into baked pie shell (I double this filling recipe and use a ten-inch pie pan). Top with whipped cream.

***

I was overjoyed when I found out that our friends Evelyn and Curtis had also been transferred to Norfolk and were, in fact, our neighbors. This was like having family together again. Sharing holidays became something that we all looked forward to, and Father's Day would never have been so special if it were not for Evelyn's "Mississippi mud." This was her all-time favorite chocolate treat. I have made it every Father's Day, not so much to honor someone's father but in memory of Evelyn.

Mississippi Mud

4 eggs
2 cups of sugar
2 sticks (½ pound) of butter (melted)
1 ½ cup of flour

⅓ cup of cocoa
1 teaspoon of vanilla
1 cup of coconut
1 cup of chopped pecans

Beat eggs and sugar until thick. Mix flour, butter, cocoa, coconut, and vanilla. Add to egg mixture. Beat well. Add nuts. Bake in greased and floured oblong pan (sheet-cake or jelly-roll pan) at 350 degrees for thirty minutes. Remove from oven and immediately spread a jar of marshmallow cream on top.

Frosting for Mississippi Mud

1 cube (¼ pound) of butter
4 tablespoons of evaporated milk
1 teaspoon of vanilla

¼ cup of cocoa
1 pound of powdered sugar
1 cup of pecan halves

Melt butter in milk. Sift cocoa and powdered sugar. Combine and add vanilla. Beat well. Spread over marshmallow cream and top with pecans.

***

In 1965, Pat received orders to Philadelphia, Pennsylvania. We've all heard it said that a sailor has a girl in every port. Well, in our case, I always seemed to be at some stage of pregnancy when we were transferred, so we liked to say that we had a baby in every port.

Our country was in the midst of the Vietnam War at that time. The United States' largest military presence in that conflict was from 1965 to 1968. Today, in South Vietnam, it is referred to as the American War. Never before in history had the media had such access to cover a war or, for that matter, all the antiwar demonstrations that were going on in our country. The civil rights movement was intensifying daily. The images of the fighting not only in Vietnam but also in our own country haunted my mind night and day.

What made it even more difficult for me was the fact that the casualties of the war who were from the East Coast were being sent to the naval hospital in South Philadelphia, which was right across the street from the navy housing where we were living. It was there that I had to go for my prenatal appointments or to take the boys to the doctor. Seeing the young men in wheelchairs, some missing limbs, became such an emotional strain on me. I would leave there in tears.

Living in navy housing again was like a shelter from the real world to us, and we were thankful to have welcoming neighbors. The first person I met was dragged to my door by her over-rambunctious son. Lucille was a fragile-looking lady in her mid-forties. She told me that she had been diagnosed with breast cancer and was undergoing treatment. I had never been around anyone with cancer, and I was very uncomfortable and unsure of what to say to her or how to act. She recognized my uneasiness and, within minutes, had put me at ease. She was quick to smile and had such a positive attitude. Before I knew it, the conversation had turned to food.

"I am making a chile relleno casserole for dinner tonight, and it is just as easy to make two, an extra one for your family," she insisted.

The closest thing to Mexican food that I had ever eaten while growing up was Truzzolino's tamales. Salvador Truzzolino made his way from Italy to Butte in the 1880s and, somewhere along the way, acquired a Philippine tamale recipe. Vendors peddled tamales through the streets of Butte by horse and wagon and delivered them to stores and restaurants in the area. Lucille questioned me about the famous Truzzolino recipe.

"All I know is that they were originally made with chicken or turkey, wrapped in corn husks, and were delicious."

"No, no." Lucille laughed. "I am talking about *real* Mexican food."

And real, hers turned out to be.

Up until that point, I had never even met a taco!

***

She later taught me how to make enchiladas. We've jokingly tagged them my "Irish enchiladas."

Lucille's Chile Relleno Casserole

In skillet, brown one pound of ground beef and half a cup of chopped onions; drain fat. Sprinkle meat with half a teaspoon of salt and a quarter teaspoon of pepper. Place one four-ounce can of whole green chilies, cut in half lengthwise, seeded, and put into a ten-by-six-and-a-half-inch baking dish. Sprinkle with one and a half cups of shredded sharp cheddar cheese. Top with meat. Arrange a one-ounce can of chopped green chilies over meat.

Combine four beaten eggs, one and a half cups of milk, a quarter cup of flour, half a teaspoon of salt, several dashes of hot pepper sauce, and a dash of pepper. Beat until smooth. Pour over chili mixture. Bake for forty-five to fifty minutes or until knife comes out clean.

Note: This is Lucille's original recipe. I add one package of taco seasoning to the ground beef.

"Irish" Enchiladas

2 8 oz. cans of tomato sauce

2 4 oz. cans of chopped green chilies

1 cup of fresh *pico de gallo*

1 can of beef consommé

1 package of taco seasoning

Cook until bubbly. Sauté two cloves of crushed garlic and one chopped onion. Add one pound of ground beef and one package of taco seasoning. Brown. Drain fat. Soften corn tortillas one at a time by briefly dropping in hot oil, just until pliable. Blot on paper towel. Place about two tablespoons of beef mixture, a little raw chopped onion, and a small amount of shredded cheddar cheese on each tortilla and roll. Pour a little sauce in the bottom of baking dish and place rolled tortillas, open side down, over sauce. Top with remaining sauce and about two cups of shredded cheddar cheese. Bake at 325 degrees for thirty minutes. Serve with extra grated cheese, sliced green onions, and sour cream.

***

On Thanksgiving Day, November 25, 1965, my labor pains started early in the day. I had never had a quick labor, so I figured I had time to cook Thanksgiving dinner. I gritted my teeth and did all the breathing exercises they taught us in Lamaze classes but barely made it through dinner.

"Time to go," I announced between contractions.

My husband gave me an ambiguous look and inquired, "Do I have time to watch *Gilligan's Island*?"

"Well, if you would like to deliver this baby during the commercials, we can give it a try."

He realized at that point that it was, in fact, time to go. He ran next door to get the babysitter for the boys, while I got myself and my suitcase into the car.

He drove to the emergency room entrance, got me out of the car and into the admissions room, and kissed me goodbye, saying as he walked out the door, "See ya tomorrow."

Maureen arrived about three hours later, just forty minutes before her grandma's birthday.

"Sorry, Grandma, we can't wait," the doctor chided as he delivered her.

Her dad had assumed that this would be an all-night saga, so he had gone home, gone to bed, and didn't meet his new daughter until the next morning.

The Saturday after Thanksgiving was the army-navy football game, which was held every year at that time in Philadelphia. The stadium was just two blocks from our navy housing. The naval hospital where I had given birth two days before was across the main street that led to the stadium. Our neighbor Carrie's baby was due the same time as ours, and when her husband had to leave for sea duty, my husband, Pat, assured him that if the baby came before he got back, we would be there to help her. Carrie called Pat early on Saturday morning to take her to the hospital. Her contractions were strong and coming close. They got as far as the first intersection, and the traffic going into the stadium was backed up for blocks.

"Looks like we'll have to walk," he informed her as he pulled the car off on a side street.

They dodged between cars to get across the street. When they made it to the sidewalk, she had to stop and hold onto the fence.

"I'm not going to make it up the hill," she panted.

"If I lift up the fence, can you crawl under?" he responded jokingly.

She was laughing and crying at the same time.

He ran ahead to the gate of the hospital, and they called for an ambulance, which couldn't get onto the street because of the traffic jam. With her arm over Pat's shoulder, he dragged her to the ambulance, and the baby arrived just as they got to the hospital. The nurse on duty was the same one who was there when Pat dropped me off two nights before.

She looked at him quizzically and asked, "Weren't you just here the other night?"

"Yeah, that was with my wife."

He had the whole staff shaking their heads in wonderment when he returned later that day with two bouquets of flowers and two boxes of chocolates.

One of Pat's shipmates was a Hispanic man, Jose Cruz. He was very impressed with my Mexican cooking. We had never done any barbecuing, so he invited us, kids and all, to a barbecue at his home. When you have four kids under eight years of age, invitations don't happen too often, so we were excited to accept. I was literally blown away by his cooking.

***

Teriyaki Steak

5 ounces of soy sauce

½ cup of cream sherry

½ cup of brown sugar

½ teaspoon of onion salt

¼ cup of vinegar

½ cup of water

½ cup of white sugar

½ teaspoon of garlic salt

¼ teaspoon of ground ginger

Marinate lean thin-sliced meat for twenty-four hours and grill.

Jose's Chicken Cacciatore

2 chickens, cut into serving pieces

½ cup of finely chopped onions

¼ cup of finely chopped green peppers

2 cloves of crushed garlic

Sauté in a quarter cup of oil until tender. Do not brown.

2 large cans (20 oz.) of tomatoes

1 bay leaf

½ teaspoon of oregano

1½ pints of chicken stock

1 teaspoon of salt

¼ teaspoon of thyme

Add to onion, green pepper, and garlic mixture and simmer for one and a half hours. Dredge chicken in seasoned flour. Fry at 365 degrees until brown. Arrange in roasting pan. Pour sauce over chicken. Cover pan and bake at 350 degrees until chicken is tender, approximately one and a half hours. Baste occasionally.

***

Jose shared his delectable barbecue sauce recipe with me. Years later, I had it featured in a restaurant, the Sportsman's Inn, in Sultan, Washington, where I worked for eleven years.

Jose's Barbecue Sauce

1 cup of ketchup

1 teaspoon of chili powder

2 dashes of Tabasco sauce

⅓ cup of Worcestershire sauce

1 teaspoon of salt

2 cups of water

Combine ingredients. bring to a boil, and let simmer for half an hour. When I make this sauce now, I add half a cup of brown sugar to give it a little sweeter taste.

Chapter 3

The bluest skies you've ever seen are in Seattle
And the green's the greenest green in Seattle . . .

When Pat received orders in early 1967, we were both elated to learn that we would be going to the West Coast.

"U.S. Naval Shipyard, Bremerton, Washington." He was beaming as he read the directive.

Moving across country with four small children might seem overwhelming to some people, but when you are military, you are somehow always prepared to be uprooted just when you begin to feel settled. There was no work involved in the packing and moving as the military takes care of it all. If you pack up Grandma's fine hand-me-down china, they will unpack it and do it over.

The biggest challenge of all was planning and packing for a four- or five-day trek with three active boys and a baby. We loaded up the big 1965 Pontiac station wagon, and we were off on another of our many family adventures. To make more room in the wagon, we strapped a couple of the suitcases to the rack on the roof. Who ever heard of seat belts?

"It's my turn to sit in the way-back!" one of the boys would howl as another was climbing over the back seat.

Pat would drive during the day, while I tried to keep the kids amused.

"Oh, we don't know where we're goin', but we're goin' just the same, and we'll follow the lead of the raggedy man who doesn't know his name," we'd sing.

I would drive at night while Pat and the kids slept. I enjoyed the peace and quiet, the calm of the night. It was like having a life free of the everyday hassle of doing dishes, chasing balls, and wiping noses. This was *my* time.

I was humming along to the soft radio music when all of a sudden, I felt a *thump, thump, thump*. As I slowed the car, I could see debris flying through the air.

"What the heck was that?" Pat hollered as he woke abruptly from his sound sleep.

I pulled the car off the highway to a stop. By now, the kids were all awake, and the baby was crying. As soon as I stepped out of the car, I saw a little hand-tooled leather belt hanging from the antenna, and I realized that my children's clothes were scattered up and down the road. It was about 2:00 a.m., so there was no traffic. I could not stop laughing as we gathered up two suitcases and as many clothes as we could find. We made room for all of it in the "way-back," where it should have been stowed in the first place.

As we were approaching Chicago on Interstate 90 about 4:00 p.m. on the second or third day of the trip, Pat, who, honestly, never complained, began grumbling.

"We're going to get stuck on this damned freeway right in the middle of the rush-hour traffic."

"Well, just take the old Whiting Road off Highway 20 when you get to East Chicago, and you don't even have to get on the freeway."

He glanced over at me quizzically and asked, "Did you see that on the map?"

"No, but it was the main road before they ever built the freeway."

"How do you know that?"

Without hesitation, I answered, "I crossed that bridge every day."

"You have never been in Chicago, Ruth. Now where did you read that information?"

I sat silently bewildered, not knowing how to answer him.

He hesitantly turned onto the road, bypassed the freeway, saved time, and avoided the traffic. We didn't discuss this matter again until later that year after seeing the movie *Bonnie and Clyde*. I was overcome by a strange feeling of nostalgia as soon as the movie started. About halfway through, I became so emotional that I had to get up and leave the theater. He was wrong. I had been in Chicago before.

After a brief visit with my folks in Butte, we continued on to Washington State. My brother had moved to Seattle in 1962, the year of the Seattle world's fair, to take a job at the Gai Brothers bakery. His family had grown quite a bit since the last time I saw them. He had five children now between the ages of fourteen and two and a half. It was like a three-ring circus when we arrived with our four kids.

I ventured to take all nine of the kids on the ferry from Seattle across the Puget Sound to Bremerton. A kindly older gentleman watched us curiously as we boarded the boat. Karen, my brother's eldest daughter, was carrying my year-and-a-half-old baby girl, and I was toting my brother's youngest boy, Jerry. As I got them all seated on a bench and handed out snacks, the old fellow approached me.

"Hey," he inquired, "are these *all* your kids?"

"Oh no, sir, the rest of them are home with their dad," I replied, trying hard to keep a straight face.

When Pat and I met with the real-estate agent in Bremerton, we made it clear to him that we needed a house as soon as possible so that we could get the kids enrolled in school. After looking at several houses, we had it narrowed down to two. The one I liked was a newer split-level house on the east side of the bridge that divides Bremerton. The one on the west side was an older home, built sometime in the 1930s. It had a full daylight basement with a room half the size of the upstairs level, which was paneled with real knotty pinewood. It was divided by large beams, with each side of the room being about twelve-by-twelve feet. It had rustic wagon-wheel chandeliers and could easily be made into two bedrooms for the boys. There was a bathroom off this room, and the remainder of the basement was a laundry room, with a chute coming from upstairs and shelves lining every wall. There were two bedrooms and a beautiful tiled bathroom upstairs, a living room, and a small dining area off the kitchen. It was a perfect family home with a huge apple tree in the yard.

I, of course, wanted the newer house. I smile now when I repeat my husband's solemn message: "There is no way we can afford a $20,000 house."

So we signed the papers and purchased what turned out to be the quaintest, most comfortable, and affordable ($13,000) home ever. We couldn't move into the house until the inspections were done and the sale finalized, but the real-estate man, who was obviously anxious to make the sale, told us that he had a furnished trailer at Lake Tahuyeh just outside of town that we could live in, rent free, while we waited.

As if six people living in a thirty-foot travel trailer was not bad enough, it rained the entire time we were there. It rained, and I cried. The more it rained, the more I cried. It rained for thirty days and thirty nights. "I hate Washington."

My husband bought an eighteen-foot fishing boat, not to take on the lake but to fish on Hood Canal. He and my brother came back after a long day of fishing with a beautiful fifteen-pound salmon.

I had dinner on the table, so I told them, "Just throw it in the bathtub, and you can clean it after dinner."

I sent the kids in to wash up, and we could hear them *ooh*-ing and *ahh*-ing over the big fish. When we finished eating, the guys headed to the bathroom to take care of their magnanimous catch.

"Oh my god," I heard Pat gasp.

It seems that my son Don had decided that a fish shouldn't be out of water, so he had filled the tub with *hot* water, and there, staring up at the proud fishermen, was a perfectly poached, *un*-gutted salmon. Well, so much for my grilled salmon recipe!

***

We moved into our new home, the rain subsided, and I decided that Washington wasn't so bad after all. The apple tree was in full bloom, and by the end of the summer, we had more apples than Johnny Appleseed could ever have envisioned. They were large red apples that, I was told when I inquired at the county fair that fall, were of the "wealthy" variety. By the end of the summer, the kids were calling me Apple Annie. The aroma of apples permeated every inch of our surroundings. I had apple butter boiling, apple pies baking, apple turnovers, apple fritters, apple crisp, and applesauce all in the making. I learned to can apple pie filling, and we had to buy an upright freezer for all my apple cakes and pies. I rightly earned my title! I am sharing with you some of my favorite apple creations.

Apple Annie's Apple Butter

16 cups of thick apple pulp   1 cup of vinegar
8 cups of sugar   4 teaspoons of cinnamon

Core and slice apples but do not peel. Add only enough water to cook apples until soft. Press through fine sieve and measure. Combine all ingredients. Cook until mixture remains in a smooth mass when a little is cooled (about one and a half hours boiling). During cooking, stir frequently to prevent burning. Pour into sterilized jars while hot and seal with canning jar lids.

Applesauce — My Way

Peel, core, and dice apples. Add a small amount of water, cover, and cook slowly until tender. Mash with potato masher. Add a few (six to eight per six medium apples) Red Hots and a cinnamon stick. Cover and let cool. Stir until candy is melted and enjoy!

This candy trick adds a special flavor to the applesauce cookies and Bernie's applesauce cake. I should mention that these apples were so naturally sweet that I did not have to add any sugar to my applesauce. Using any variety of apple, I make it the same way today.

***

Applesauce Cookies

1 cup of shortening
1 teaspoon of soda
2 cups of brown sugar (packed)
1 teaspoon of salt
2 eggs
1 teaspoon of cinnamon
½ cup of cold coffee
1 teaspoon of nutmeg
2 cups of well-drained thick applesauce
3 ½ cups of flour
1 teaspoon of cloves
½ cup of coarsely chopped nuts
1 cup of raisins

Mix shortening, sugar, and eggs. Stir in coffee and applesauce. Mix dry ingredients and stir into applesauce mixture. Chill at least two hours. Drop by tablespoons two inches apart on lightly greased cookie sheet. Bake at four hundred degrees for nine to twelve minutes. Frost if desired with a butter icing.

Apple Crisp

Place 4 cups of peeled, sliced apples in buttered ten-by-six-by-two-inch baking dish. Sprinkle with the following:

1 teaspoon of cinnamon
½ teaspoon of salt
¼ cup of water

Rub together the following:

¾ cup of flour
1 cup of brown sugar
⅓ cup of butter

Drop mixture over apples. Bake at 350 degrees for forty minutes. Serve warm with cream.

Apple Muffins

2 cups of sifted flour
4 teaspoons of baking powder
½ teaspoon of salt
¾ teaspoon of cinnamon
¼ teaspoon of nutmeg

1 beaten egg
1 cup of milk
⅓ cup of melted shortening
¾ cup of chopped apples
¼ cup of sugar

Sift dry ingredients. Combine egg, milk, and shortening. Add liquid to dry ingredients all at once; stir until mixed. Add apples. Fill greased muffin pans two-thirds full. Bake at four hundred degrees for twenty-five minutes. Makes a dozen muffins.

Apple Dapple Cake

3 eggs
3 cups of flour
2 cups of white sugar
1 teaspoon of salt
1 cup of oil
1 teaspoon of baking soda
2 teaspoons of vanilla
1 teaspoon of baking powder
3 cups of peeled, chopped raw apples
1 teaspoon of cinnamon
1 cup of chopped walnuts

Beat eggs, sugar, oil, and vanilla. Add dry ingredients and mix well. Fold in chopped apples and nuts. Bake in greased and floured tube or Bundt pan at 350 degrees for an hour and fifteen minutes. Glaze while cake is still warm.

Glaze:

Bring the following to a boil over medium heat:

½ cup of brown sugar
½ cube of butter
½ cup of evaporated milk or heavy cream

Pour over warm cake.

***

By the time school started in the fall, we were well settled into our new home. Having lived in navy housing, the boys were never able to have a pet, so their dad promised that when we got our own home, they could choose a pet.

"How about a dog?" chimed Raymond, who was four years old.

That sounded good to me as I am not a cat person. We ended up with a German Shepard, a white Persian cat with one blue eye and one green eye, and my favorite pet of all time, Ralph, the alligator. When Ralph outgrew the stainless-steel galley serving tray that was his bed, we had no choice but to keep him in the bathtub at night. The kids would take him outside to play during the day, to the delight of all the neighbors.

I had a man knock at the door one day and ask me very seriously, "Do you have an alligator in your bathtub?"

I told him with the straightest face I could muster, "Yes, sir, I do. And when I want to take a bath, I just say, 'Move over, Ralph.'"

He walked away, shaking his head.

We only had Ralph for about a year. He quit eating and wasn't very active, so I took him to the local veterinarian. The vet was a quiet, serious older man who had given our dog and cat their shots. He and his attendant smiled as I walked in, neither of them being able to see over the counter what was at the end of my dog leash. Only when the dogs and cats in the waiting room began a huge barking, howling, hissing ruckus did he realize that this was no everyday pet. He took us to a room immediately, baffled and not knowing what to tell me.

Scratching his head, he apologetically said, "I am so sorry, but I was not trained to treat alligators. Perhaps you should contact the reptile garden at the Seattle Zoo."

If only we had the ability at that time to "Google it." He gave me vitamin drops of some kind, told me not to give Ralph any raw meat, and charged me $40. We lost our beloved pet a few days later. The kids gave him a proper burial in the backyard, under the apple tree. The dog and the cat both mourned with us.

The boys started school, and I took a job at the Sears Service Center near our home. I hired a lady who was referred to me by my neighbor, Sandy, to babysit my daughter for the five hours a day I worked. What a perfect job. I would get the boys off to school in the morning, deliver Maureen to Clara, be at work by 9:00 a.m., and be home for an hour before school got out. It was almost as if the boys didn't even know I worked. Clara had older children, both in high school, and when she and Maureen met, it was love at first sight. Maureen called her "my lovey" and would beg to go to see her on my weekends off.

The boys kept me busy with sports, Cub Scouts, swimming classes, band, and youth bowling league on Saturday mornings. I was a scout den mother, and I ran the concession stand for the little league and taught CCD on Sunday. My Crock-Pot became my best friend. My neighbor gave me a cookbook, *The Working Wife's Cookbook* (Crown Publishers, New York, 1963). Her inscription on the inside cover read, "Ruth — To you and the kids, etc., etc., etc., and 'the old man.' Stuffed green peppers!" The pages of this book are stained and tattered after fifty years of steady use.

***

Stuffed Peppers

Unlike most stuffed peppers, this recipe calls for top-of-the-stove cooking and can be prepared the night before and refrigerated until time to cook them. I have also done them in the Crock-Pot.

4 large firm green peppers	2 teaspoons of salt
1 pound of ground beef	¼ teaspoon of Tabasco
¼ cup of uncooked rice	3 tablespoons of cold water
3 onions, 1 grated and 2 sliced	3 tablespoons of salad oil
1 egg, slightly beaten	1 can (1 lb.) of stewed tomatoes
¼ cup of honey	¼ cup of lemon juice

Put the peppers in a large pot, cover with water, and bring to a boil. When water reaches boiling point, turn off the heat and let peppers stay in the water for five minutes. Drain and cool. Cut the top inch off the peppers and save. Remove the seeds and the membranes and rinse. Grate one onion; mix with the beef, rice, beaten egg, salt, Tabasco, and three tablespoons of cold water. Stuff the peppers with mixture and replace tops. Heat salad oil in the pot in which the peppers were scalded. Sauté the two sliced onions in the oil until golden but not crisp. Add the stewed tomatoes and then place the peppers (with their tops put back on) over the sauce. Spoon some of the sauce over the peppers. Cover the pot and simmer over a low heat for thirty minutes. Add honey and lemon juice to the sauce and stir well. Cook for another thirty minutes. You can also add a little more salt and pepper to taste at this time. This is still one of my favorite dinners. Great served with creamed corn.

***

I have a feeling that the cookies that Clara made for my daughter were a recipe of her own making. I had never heard of a gumdrop cookie. They were very much like an oatmeal cookie but with coconut and gumdrops. The kids loved them.

Clara's Gumdrop Cookies

1 cup of shortening	2 cups of sifted flour
1 cup of brown sugar	1 teaspoon of baking soda
1 cup of white sugar	1 teaspoon of baking powder
2 eggs	¼ teaspoon of salt
1 teaspoon of vanilla	1 cup of nuts
1 cup of coconut	1 cup of gumdrops
2 cups of quick oatmeal	

Cream shortening and sugars. Add eggs and vanilla and beat. Sift dry ingredients and stir in. Add remaining ingredients. Drop by spoonful on ungreased cookie sheet. Bake at 375 degrees for ten minutes.

***

My job at the Sears Service Department consisted of scheduling service calls, renewing service contracts, filling parts orders for the service men, and handling the front counter. When the Sears West Coast Division announced a contest for the service employee who sold the most laundry detergent, I quickly jumped at the challenge. Everybody needs soap, so how difficult could it be to sell it to everyone who called in for appliance service?

"Yes, ma'am, he'll be out to service your washing machine on Tuesday morning, between nine-thirty and ten o'clock. I'd be happy to have him bring you a twenty-five-pound box of our laundry detergent. It's on special this week, and I can just add it to your account with your service charge."

No one ever seemed to tell me no. When I would call to renew their service contracts, I would ask them what kind of detergent they used and then explain to them how much better our biodegradable brand was for their washing machine. I personally didn't care for the damned soap. I made up a little ditty that I would sing to the service guys who were not all too happy with my phenomenal sales since it meant that they had to load the bulky soap boxes into their trucks every day. "Sears's detergent—it doesn't get your clothes very clean, but it sure is good for your washing machine."

I won the contest hands down. Easiest $50 I ever made! For my birthday that year, I received from my devoted crew a hundred-pound barrel of Sears laundry detergent tied with a big red bow.

My niece Sheri came to live with us in Bremerton to attend Olympic College, which was just a few blocks from our house. She went to school during the day and worked the graveyard shift at the Puget Sound Naval Shipyard. She was extremely adept at computer work and very ambitious. She had, however, lived a sheltered and what I would call a deprived life. Her mother was killed in a tragic car accident in Butte in 1959 when Sheri was eleven years old, leaving seven motherless children. Their father was in the army. He was arranging to have four family members each take a couple of the kids when his aunt Bernice showed up from Oregon.

"Bill, you cannot separate these children after the trauma they have just gone through losing their mother," she chastised him.

So at sixty-seven years of age, she retired from her career at Stanford University and took all the kids to assure that they would be together.

Bill eventually remarried. Their new stepmother was from Korea, spoke no English, and had to be very overwhelmed not only by the lifestyle in America but also with the responsibility of caring for seven children, aged twelve to three years old. I can only imagine her despair and frustration. This does not justify to me, however, the physical, verbal, and emotional abuse that the children endured over the years. Sheri's self-esteem was so damaged, she didn't even know how to laugh. She reminded me recently that she didn't know what an avocado was nor ever had a banana split before she came to live with me. She had also never had any positive encouragement, so she had a dreadful inferiority complex. One day, when she was walking down the street, a carload of boys drove by and whistled at her. She came home in tears, thinking that they were making fun of her. I assured her that they were admiring the fact that she was a very shapely, attractive young lady.

She started going to church with us on Sundays. This was all new to her; she had never been to church. This was the 1960s, and the hippie era was in full swing. Our church choir had organized a group to perform a folk mass. You know, the guitars and the "Kumbaya." Sheri, who was once told in grammar school that she could hold the star in the Christmas pageant so that she wouldn't sing, was now performing folk music and playing the guitar in the choir. It was heartwarming for me to see her socializing and making friends.

Although she hadn't learned to cook, she decided that she wanted to make a lemon Jell-O cake for an upcoming fund-raiser at the church. When her first baking venture came out of the oven slightly tilted, she was devastated.

"I'm not taking it to church," she informed me.

"Oh yes, you are," I sharply responded. "You made it as your offering, and just because it is not perfect is no reason for you not to share it."

She was visibly disgruntled with me as I carried the lopsided cake into church. It was the second item to sell, and I think it was a lesson for her about carrying through on a commitment.

By the time Thanksgiving rolled around, she was ready to try her hand once again at baking. She made a delicious pumpkin chiffon pie. The recipe is not included in this book, however, as she loaned out my recipe, and it was never returned. Yes, she is still hearing about it today! She fell in love and had her heart broken, which actually broke my heart as well. It was finally time for her to get on with her life, and when she left home, I cried for three days.

She, in the course of time, married and had two beautiful children, John and Jamie. She and her husband fostered many children over the years. They are now proud grandparents of seven and are honored to call another seventeen from their foster children their grandbabies also. Sheri remains as close to my heart as any daughter could be.

Chapter 4

Aloha i ko makou hale.

As a young girl, I dreamed of one day strolling along a sandy beach, watching the waves roll in, and feeling the sea breeze brush my cheeks and ruffle my hair.

"How would you like to move to Hawaii?" came the hyped-up voice of my husband over the phone.

My answer didn't come easily. Take the kids out of school, quit my job, and leave our home? My head was spinning, but my pounding heart was screaming, "Yes, yes!"

I tried to answer calmly, "Well, we'd better give it some serious thought."

It had been easy to move every four years when the kids were younger, but the boys were involved so much in school now, and my baby would be starting kindergarten soon. My decision was made quickly, however, when he told me that he had received his orders and he would have to go with or without us. I was reluctant to discuss it with the boys, but as soon as I said "Hawaii," they were all ready to pack their bags.

"Wow, can we surf?" squealed Don.

My eldest son would be starting his first year of high school in the fall, and I was concerned that a move at this time would be difficult for him. He set my mind at ease by telling me that he was actually ready for a change, and it wouldn't be any different starting a new school there than it would be starting in a new high school in Bremerton. So "not to worry, Mother."

Many years later, he shared with me his theory that military kids adjust easier to change and have the ability to make friends quite effortlessly. He also confided that even as an adult, he was ready to move every four years. I made arrangements to rent the house to a couple who were both teachers at Olympic College. The navy would move all our household goods and furniture and ship our car. Plans were in place, and we were all very excited to embark on yet another exciting adventure.

Whenever I see someone traveling with more than one child, I shake my head in wonderment. Keeping track of three rambunctious boys at an international airport is not exactly a piece of cake. Add to that a crying toddler who, thirty miles across the Pacific Ocean, realized that she left her security blanket in her uncle's car and loudly demands that they turn the plane around and go back . . . *now!*

After I got her calmed down, Maureen leaned over the seat in front of us and made friends with a lovely middle-aged lady who was traveling alone. After a few minutes of chitchat, I politely ended the conversation as I didn't want her to be a pest. We were all soon settled in for our long flight. I was so proud that my boys were so well behaved and my precious girl was sleeping peacefully.

I dozed off but woke abruptly, hearing a little commotion. The "lovely lady" in front of us let out a shriek just as I pulled my daughter back from the top of her seat, and lo and behold, in her little hand was a very well-coiffed blond wig. I was, of course, mortified, and the people around us were obviously amused. As I sheepishly handed her hairpiece back to her, I was saying a thank-you to someone out there that I would never have to face this "lovely lady" again. As fate would have it, this would not be the case.

When we landed safely in Honolulu, my husband, along with several other military men, were all waiting anxiously to greet their families. The "lovely lady" exited just ahead of us and was met by a very distinguished-looking gentleman. My husband was eager to introduce me to this man, who happened to be his commanding officer. I could feel the flush on my face and see the boys giggling as the introductions began.

I already knew that the captain's name was O'Neill, so after shaking his hand, I addressed his "lovely" wife. "Oh, so you are the other Mrs. O'Neill."

She glared at me, expressionless, and said dryly, "No, dear, *you* are the *other* Mrs. O'Neill."

To make an uncomfortable moment even more distressful, Maureen tugged on her skirt, looked up at her, smiled, and chirped, "Daddy, this is my new friend."

The "lovely lady" did respond with a smile.

Welcome to Hawaii. Aloha nui loa.

We were assigned to navy housing near Pearl Harbor, Hokulani Heights. Our house was a four-bedroom, two-and-a-half-bath, two-story unit with a huge laundry room and a beautiful covered lanai through the sliding glass doors off the living room. The grounds around the buildings were all professionally landscaped, and we had a magnificent palm tree in the backyard. This was truly paradise.

The grammar school was within walking distance of the house, and the kids were anxious to make new friends. We decided to enroll Patrick in the boys' Catholic high school, Damien, in Honolulu. He had to take several tests to be accepted. The school is in an exclusive upscale section of town, and we had to provide his transportation.

On the day that he enrolled, we were standing in the office, talking with one of the receptionists, and heard a booming, very familiar voice with a distinct Irish brogue, ring out, "Ruthie Keane!"

I turned in shock, hearing my maiden name, and before I could even react, I was enveloped in the arms of Brother O'Donnell, the Irish Christian brother who had been my Irish dance instructor in high school. This was, yet again, another of my "small world" experiences.

We were elated to see each other after so many years and so far from home. I could hardly contain my excitement as I introduced him to my handsome, very blond, six-foot-tall son. Being blond at Damien High School, I might mention, was as obvious as being a petunia in a pumpkin patch. Probably 90 percent of the boys enrolled there are of Asian or Polynesian decent, the remaining being of mixed heritage, predominately dark complexioned.

After his first week there, Patrick informed me, "Boy, Mom, now I know how the black people in the South felt when they were discriminated against."

He promptly learned the meaning of *houli*, and if he had not been such an outgoing, self-assured kid, he may have felt that he was being bullied. He did well scholastically and excelled in sports. He made the school baseball team and pitched their way to the championship finals.

As if it were just yesterday, I vividly remember walking my baby girl to her first day of kindergarten. The boys skipped ahead, excited about their new school and meeting new friends. I lollygagged behind, holding tightly to her hand, knowing that I had to soon let go. When we arrived, there was a frightened little boy sobbing and hanging on tightly to his mother. Maureen pulled away from me quickly and went to his side to comfort him. She was such a sweet, compassionate child. His mother's eyes met mine, and we both began to cry. I cried all the way home.

Dan and Maureen became best friends. His mom and I met for coffee the next day and remained close friends until she passed away in

2012. Ethel had worked for the government in Washington, D.C., before her marriage. She was older and wiser, and I respected and admired her and so enjoyed her company. She was quiet and serious and was constantly amused at my happy-go-lucky attitude about life. She often compared me to Erma Bombeck. She encouraged me to enroll in the adult classes at the University of Hawaii, for which I have always been grateful. She was the ultimate June Cleaver—housewife, mother, and cook—and she loved sharing recipes and trying new foods. My recipe file overflows with Ethel's culinary expertise.

She would tell people on their birthday, "In honor of your birthday, I ate a cake."

One of the first things she ever shared with me was her delectable chocolate cookie sheet cake. I wish that I had a dollar for every time I have made this cake over the years. I didn't have the heart to tell her, though, that I do not like chocolate.

***

Ethel's Chocolate Cookie Sheet Cake

Sift into bowl the following:

2 cups of flour   2 cups of sugar
½ teaspoon of salt

Put in saucepan the following:

1 cube of butter (¼ lb.)   1 cup of water
½ cup of shortening   3 tablespoons of cocoa

Bring to a boil and pour over flour mixture and mix well.

In another bowl, beat two eggs and add the following:

1 teaspoon of baking soda
1 teaspoon of vanilla
½ cup of buttermilk (sweet milk can be substituted)

Beat well and add to other mixture. Bake in greased and floured fifteen-and-a-half-by-ten-and-a-half-by-one-inch sheet pan. Bake for twenty minutes at 350 degrees.

Icing for Chocolate Cookie Sheet Cake

Start icing during the last five minutes of baking cake. Use the same saucepan as for cake. Melt but do not boil one cube of butter (one quarter pound). Remove from heat and add the following:

1 pound of powdered sugar
3 tablespoons of cocoa
4 tablespoons of milk
1 teaspoon of vanilla
½ cup of chopped nuts (optional)

Stir well and frost while cake is still hot.

***

I have always liked scalloped potatoes, but until I ate Ethel's scalloped potatoes supreme, I couldn't relate to a delicious potato. This is an extraordinary hot dish for a potluck.

Scalloped Potatoes Supreme

½ cup of evaporated milk
8 to 10 potatoes, sliced
1 large green pepper, chopped
Salt and pepper to taste

1 can of cream-of-mushroom soup
1 large onion, chopped
1 medium carrot, grated
Parmesan cheese and cheddar cheese

Brown onion, green pepper, and carrot slightly. Combine with soup and milk. Heat sauce (don't boil). Arrange layers, beginning with the sauce, potatoes, Parmesan cheese, and cheddar cheese in buttered casserole dish. Continue to layer until all ingredients are used. Top with extra cheddar cheese. Cover and bake in 350-degree oven for forty-five minutes. Uncover and bake twenty minutes more until brown. Makes about eight servings. *Yummy!*

Ethel's Pumpkin Bread

1 ⅔ cups of flour
1 ½ cups of sugar
¼ teaspoon of baking powder
1 teaspoon of baking soda
¾ teaspoon of salt
1 cup of chopped nuts
½ teaspoon of nutmeg

½ cup of salad oil
½ cup of water
1 cup of canned mashed pumpkin
2 eggs
1 cup of chopped dates
½ teaspoon of cloves
½ teaspoon of cinnamon

Sift together dry ingredients. In a bowl, beat eggs slightly. Add oil, water, and pumpkin and mix together. Blend dry ingredients into egg mixture. Add dates and nuts and fold in. Bake in greased loaf pan at 350 degrees for about one and a half hours.

***

The next recipe is quite unique. Ethel always made it with fresh grated coconut, but it is also good made with canned or packaged coconut although not as moist.

Coconut Dessert Loaf

6 cups of flour
2 cups of sugar
2 tablespoons of baking powder
1 teaspoon of salt
2 cups of milk
2 eggs (beaten)
4 teaspoons of vanilla
2 ⅔ cups of fresh shredded coconut (can substitute canned or packaged)
2 6 oz. packages (2 cups) of semisweet chocolate chips

Preheat oven to 350 degrees. In large bowl, combine flour, sugar, baking powder, and salt; mix thoroughly. Stir in coconut and semisweet chocolate chips. Combine milk, eggs, and vanilla. Add to dry ingredients and stir until well blended. Let stand twenty minutes. Spread into two well-greased nine-by-five-by-three-inch loaf pans. Bake at 350 degrees for an hour and five minutes. Cool and remove from pans. Makes two loaves.

***

The name says "easy," and this pie is as quick and easy as any dessert you will ever make.

Green Easy Pie

Make your own one-crust pie shell and cool or use a ready-made crust.

Mix in bowl the following:

1 can of sweetened condensed milk
½ cup of fresh lime juice
1 10 oz. can of crushed pineapple (drained)
A couple of drops of green food coloring

Put mixture in pie shell. Refrigerate for three hours. Serve with whipped cream. Garnish with shaved chocolate if desired.

***

Raymond's second grade teacher was a delightful young Polynesian girl, Ms. Ann Ohara. All her students loved her. She would take treats to school on special occasions, usually conventional Hawaiian foods. It was important to her that the kids learned the history and traditions of the islands. Raymond learned to eat poi, and at eight years old, he knew how to dig an imu to roast a whole pig. Ms. Ohara shared several of her recipes with me.

Ms. Ohara's Pineapple Bars

2 cups of granulated sugar
1 ½ cups of flour
½ cup of butter
½ teaspoon of salt
4 eggs
½ teaspoon of baking soda
1 20 oz. can of crushed pineapple, well drained
1 cup of chopped walnuts

Melt butter. Add sugar. Beat eggs well and add to mixture. Add pineapple, nuts, and dry ingredients. Bake in greased ten-and-a-half-by-fifteen-by-two-inch pan at 350 degrees for forty to forty-five minutes.

Hawaiian Carrot Bread

Sift flour, salt, soda, and cinnamon together. Make a well in the mixing bowl with the dry ingredients. Add nuts, oil, vanilla, sugar, eggs, carrots, and raisins. Mix well and pour into well-greased loaf pan. Let stand for two minutes before baking. Bake at 350 degrees for one hour. Cool before slicing to prevent crumbling.

***

This recipe for Hawaiian fruitcake makes the best fruitcake I have ever eaten. Must have something to do with the macadamia nuts. It gets even better if you wrap it in brandy-soaked cheesecloth and keep it in an airtight container.

Mea Ono Ai Hawaii

¾ cup of all-purpose flour
¼ teaspoon of baking powder
¼ teaspoon of baking soda
¾ teaspoon of salt
¾ cup of granulated sugar
2 cups (10 oz.) of whole dates
2 cups of whole macadamia nuts
1 cup (8 oz.) of glazed natural pineapple pieces
3 eggs
½ teaspoon of brandy flavoring

Combine flour, baking powder, baking soda, and salt. Stir in sugar. Add dates, macadamia nuts, and pineapple pieces. Stir to coat with flour mixture. Beat eggs until foamy and light yellow (about three minutes). Stir eggs and brandy flavoring into fruit-flour mixture. Mix well. Pour into greased and wax-paper-lined nine-by-five-by-three-inch loaf pan. Bake in three-hundred-degree oven for one and a half hours. Cool in pan for ten minutes. Remove from pan, peel off paper, and finish cooling on wire rack. Excellent sliced thin. Keeps well, tightly wrapped, for up to two months.

***

Shortly after we got settled into our new home, a neighbor, Cora, showed up at the door with a cake to welcome us. I was so impressed by her gesture and by the cake that I have used this recipe to welcome new neighbors whenever I can. I call it my "welcome" cake.

Cora's Banana Cake

1 ½ cups of sugar
1 cup of mayonnaise
¾ cup of mashed bananas
1 teaspoon of vanilla
⅛ teaspoon of salt
2 ½ cups of flour
2 teaspoons of baking soda dissolved in ¾ cup of warm coffee

Mix all ingredients together. Bake in greased thirteen-by-ten-inch pan at 350 degrees for approximately one hour. Cool and sprinkle with sifted powdered sugar.

***

Having fresh pineapple readily available was a real treat for me. I was anxious to make my pineapple upside-down cake, which, up until now, I had only made with canned pineapple. The recipe I use was originally for peach upside-down cake and is delicious made with either fruit, but fresh pineapple is definitely the way to go.

Pineapple Velvet Upside-Down Cake

2 tablespoons of butter   ½ cup of light brown sugar (packed)

Arrange sliced fresh pineapple or peaches to cover bottom of pan. Place Maraschino cherry halves in center or around fruit.

1 ⅓ cups of flour   1 teaspoon of baking powder
¾ cup of sugar   ¾ cup of milk
¼ cup of butter (softened)   1 egg
1 teaspoon of vanilla

Melt two tablespoons of butter over low heat in a nine-inch round or square pan (I use a square cast-iron skillet). Sprinkle brown sugar over butter and arrange fruit slices and cherries. Mix flour, baking powder, half a cup of the milk, butter, eggs, and vanilla. Beat at medium speed with mixer for one minute. Add remaining milk and continue beating for half a minute. Pour mixture over fruit. Bake in 350-degree oven for forty minutes. Invert on serving plate as soon as it comes out of oven.

***

Our first Christmas on the island was a glorious one. I made all the kids Christmas stockings with their names and "Mele Kalikimaka" on them. It thrills me to know that a couple of them still hang these stockings every year. My Christmas cookie baking marathon usually started on December 15, which was Don's birthday and traditionally the day we would get our Christmas tree. Live trees were very expensive, having to be transported from the mainland, but I would not settle for anything else.

As we were setting up our first Hawaiian Christmas tree, our next-door neighbor, Helen, brought us cookies that I had never heard of but have become one of my favorite holiday treats. Helen had a very dry sense of humor, and it clearly comes through reading this recipe, which I am sure she had tweaked to her own liking. I'm going to write it just as she did.

Helen's Christmas Cookies

½ pound of hazelnuts, grated (without shells)
½ pound of butter
½ pound of sugar (1 cup)
1 egg
½ pound of flour (2 cups)

Cream butter, sugar, and egg. Add flour. Blend in nuts and "rum it up" to taste. Form in rolls and refrigerate until firm. Slice and bake in slow oven (300 to 325 degrees) until edges turn light brown.

***

I pleaded with my dad to come to Hawaii to visit us, but his answer was always the same. "As soon as they build the bridge, I'll be there."

He bought my mom and her retired schoolteacher friend, Edna, tickets for a Hawaiian vacation. We had three glorious weeks of jaunting around the island, enjoying all the tourist sights. Watching my mother and Edna paddle kayaks on Waikiki, sing on the stage with Don Ho, dance the hula, tour the Polynesian Cultural Center, and weep at the memorial held on the USS *Arizona* brought me joy beyond words.

My mother was in awe of Waimea Falls. I remember her looking over the viewing platform, whispering, "This is probably as close to heaven as I'll ever get."

My dad must have been so impressed with mother's stories and fabulous photos that he had second thoughts about waiting for the bridge. When I spoke with him on the phone, I told him that if he would come visit, I would make him a coconut cream pie every day that he stayed. He laughed and said, "We'll see," but I never really expected him to ever get on a plane.

One day he and my mom were downtown and walked past the travel agency.

"Come on, Mary, let's check out the flights to Honolulu."

My mother was as shocked as I was when she called to tell me that they were coming for a visit. For all his fear of flying, that turned out to be the most exciting part of the trip for him. He talked about it to whoever would listen.

We had a glorious month, repeating all the wondrous things we had done the year before. Being true to my promise, I got up before everyone every morning and shredded fresh right-off-our-tree coconut to make my daddy's pie. The first day, everyone was delighted. With eight people, however, the slices were quite thin. By the end of the week, not everyone was eating pie, so there was a little left over every day. By the second week, we were taking pie to the neighbors.

"Enough," my dad dissuaded me.

"A promise is a promise" was my snappy comeback, and I continued my daily baking.

He probably never ate coconut cream pie again after he left Hawaii.

***

Fresh Coconut Cream Pie

1 cup of sugar

¼ teaspoon of salt

3 egg yolks, beaten

1 cup of heavy cream

½ teaspoon of almond extract

½ cup of cornstarch

2 cups of grated fresh coconut

3 cups of hot milk

1 teaspoon of vanilla extract

Prepare and bake one nine-inch pie shell. Let cool completely before filling. Combine sugar, cornstarch, and salt; gradually add to milk in medium saucepan, stirring until smooth. Bring to boiling, stirring, over medium heat; boil two minutes. Remove from heat. Stir half of hot mixture into egg yolks and then combine with the rest in saucepan. Cook, stirring over low heat, until it boils and is thick enough to mound from spoon—about five minutes. Turn into bowl; stir in extracts and half of the coconut. Place waxed paper directly on filling; refrigerate for one hour. Turn into pie shell; refrigerate for three hours. Whip cream and spread over filling; top with remaining coconut.

Note: I usually use one and a half cups of the coconut in the filling and top with the remaining half cup. You can use canned or packaged coconut in place of the grated fresh coconut.

***

My dad always loved my cooking, and when I served him Eli's Swedish meatballs, he informed my mom that maybe they should just stay in Hawaii. As I mentioned in the first chapter, she was not the greatest cook. She did take the recipe when they left and promised me that she would make them for him. I doubt that she ever did.

The following recipes came from my neighbor Sharon. They were handed down to her by her Swedish grandmother. Sharon's husband was a "lifer," as the guys called anyone who stayed in the navy for over twenty years. They were quite the couple. He was old enough to be her father, short and stocky, and never had much to say. She was tall, almost six feet, and always looked like she just stepped out of a fashion magazine. She was raised in Los Angeles by her grandmother. Her mother made her living traveling with a carnival and became a seasoned shortchange artist. They lived in an apartment over a liquor store, and the owner of the store, after being shortchanged several times, would tell her to just take whatever she was going to buy rather than take money from her and have to make change.

Eli's Swedish Meatballs

4 tablespoons of butter
⅓ cup of minced onion
1 egg
½ cup of milk
½ cup of fresh bread crumbs
¼ pound of ground pork
1 cup of water
¾ cup of light cream

2 teaspoons of salt
3 teaspoons of sugar
½ teaspoon of allspice
¼ teaspoon of nutmeg
1 pound of ground chuck
3 tablespoons of flour
⅛ teaspoon of pepper

In two tablespoons of hot butter, sauté onion until golden. Meanwhile, in large mixing bowl, beat egg; add milk and bread crumbs. Let stand for five minutes. Add one teaspoon of salt, two teaspoons of sugar, allspice, nutmeg, meats, and onion. Blend well with a fork. In the same skillet, heat two tablespoons of butter. Using two teaspoons of meat, shape mixture into small balls. Drop into skillet; brown well on all sides. Remove to warm casserole. Repeat until all meat balls are browned. Into fat in skillet, stir flour, one teaspoon of sugar, and one teaspoon of salt and pepper. Slowly add the water and cream. Stir until thickened. Serve meatballs in gravy.

Fresh Peach Crumble

In a ten-by-six-by-two-inch baking dish, combine the following:

4 cups of sliced fresh peaches
½ cup of sugar
2 tablespoons of quick-cooking tapioca
⅛ teaspoon of salt
1 teaspoon of fresh lemon juice

Blend together to coarse crumb consistency:

½ cup of flour
¼ cup of dark brown sugar, firmly packed
¼ cup of butter

Pat uniformly over top of fruit mixture. Cover. Bake fifteen minutes at 375 degrees. Remove cover and bake thirty to forty minutes more. If desired, garnish with whipped cream and uncooked fresh peach slices.

***

My dad was enjoying his Hawaiian vacation. He would get up early every morning, sit on the lanai, and read the newspaper while having his coffee.

One morning, as my mother and I were planning our excursion for the day, he interrupted us, inquiring in a quizzical tone of voice, "Mary, where is your yet?"

"My what?" Mother responded.

He repeated the question, this time asking, "Where is a woman's 'yet'?"

Mother gave me a wondering glance. "Do you know what he is talking about?" she asked me.

"No," I replied.

"Well, it says right here that this man shot his wife, and the bullet is in her yet."

I was sad when the day came for them to end their vacation. I will forever treasure the memories of the time they spent with us, and my dad talked about it for the rest of his life.

Raymond was in the third grade at this time. He received an invitation to a birthday slumber party. As I read the invitation, I realized that my children had never been away from home overnight, and I panicked. My first reaction was "Absolutely no. I don't even know these people."

The neighbor boys were also invited, and their mother, Helen, assured me that it was okay. "His dad is an officer, and they live off base in a beautiful home in a very posh neighborhood near Diamond Head," she affirmed.

I didn't care where they lived or what rank his father was. I couldn't wrap my head around letting him go.

"Call and talk to the kid's mom," my husband suggested.

I thought about it long and hard and finally decided to call. She was very pleasant and excited about the party and put my mind at ease. I ended up sending him off with a smile, but I didn't sleep all night.

He came home the next day with a big brown grocery bag full of avocados.

"Where did you get those?" I questioned him.

"From Gomer Pyle" was his quick response.

I laughed and repeated my question.

"Gomer Pyle lives right next door to my friend's house, and he has a whole orchard of avocado trees, and he told us that we could have as many as we wanted."

Where did my son learn the word *orchard*, and why in the world would he think that man was Gomer Pyle?

I had come to find out from my neighbor that Jim Nabors did live next door to Raymond's friend in an elegant one-hundred-year-old plantation-style home, surrounded by avocado trees. The next time Raymond was invited to go there, I suggested that if he picked avocados again, he should ask Mr. Nabors to sign the paper bag for me. He did, and he did. I was so thrilled to have his autograph. I was hoping that I would someday get to meet him, but he passed away at eighty-seven years of age just last year. His voice was as strong and clear at 84 as it was when he was a young man. He sang the opening theme, "Back Home Again in Indiana" for the 2014 Indianapolis 500 race in his home state.

***

Now what was I to do with all these avocados? Guacamole—lots of guacamole! Sounds good, except I had no idea how to make guacamole. I diced and mashed and tasted and finally just gave up. I eventually met a man who was a cook on a cruise ship, and he shared this delectable version of guacamole with me. It is the best I've ever tasted.

Guacamole

6 avocados

2 onions

6 or 8 jalapeños (to taste)

Fresh cilantro

6 ripe tomatoes

Chili peppers

2 fresh-squeezed lemons

Peel, seed, and chop avocado. Chop tomatoes and onions and chili peppers. Chop jalapeños, extracting all the seeds. Mix all ingredients and put in blender for just a few seconds. Season to taste. Add fresh lemon juice, which will help keep the color and give it that wonderful lemony aftertaste.

***

There was a large tree in the field behind our house. I'm not sure what kind of tree it was. My son Don, who was thirteen years old, and my nephew Jim, seventeen, who was staying with us at the time, decided to build a tree house. They hoisted a large piece of plywood to a limb that was at least fifteen feet off the ground and attached a rope to pull themselves up and slide down.

Once they were up on their platform, the two-hundred-pound Samoan brothers who lived next door grabbed hold of the rope and began swinging on it. I didn't hear the crash, but the screams that followed could have probably been heard for a mile away. Running toward the sliding glass door, I could see the broken limbs shattered on the ground and both boys trying, unable, to get off the ground.

Now my screaming was louder than theirs, and some of the neighbors were running toward the tree. Someone helped Don to his feet, and I could see both his hands hanging parallel to his arms—a complete impact fracture of the radius and ulna, both bones in both wrists. He was white as a ghost, not crying or speaking. Someone was holding him as I was helping Jim up. I realized that one of the bones in Jim's left arm was protruding. Why hadn't someone called the aid car?

I screamed for my neighbor Sharon to please drive me to the hospital. She kept telling me that she couldn't, but I wasn't going to take no for an answer. With the help of a neighbor, we got the boys in Sharon's car. I sat in the back with Don. I know now that we were both in shock. Someone had wrapped Jim's hand with a towel, and he was in the front seat with Sharon.

"Aunt Ruth, I can't feel my hand," I heard him sob.

I was begging Sharon to drive faster.

It was about two miles to the naval hospital. Thankfully, it was a Sunday evening, so the traffic was not a problem. She pulled into the emergency entrance and ran for help, leaving me in the car with the boys, who were both completely silent. I could feel my heart pounding but was trying to stay calm. Two medics came running out, along with a doctor, who had a full leg cast.

Sharon broke down into sobs and confessed to me that the reason she had first refused to drive was because she had been drinking all day. Only then did I realize that she was very inebriated.

Without any questions or even paperwork, they rushed Jim to the operating room.

As they were rolling Don into the elevator on a gurney, the doctor looked at me and inquired, "Are you okay?"

I was shaking uncontrollably, but I managed to answer, "Yes, I'm fine."

His next question was "Where are your shoes?"

I didn't realized that I had not taken time to put my shoes on when we left the house.

In the room next to us was an eighteen-year-old boy who had been brought in earlier that day with two broken wrists also. He had broken his lifting weights. Three boys, six "silver-fork deformity" breaks. This term is used to describe the peculiar appearance of the hand when it is displaced by a distal radius fracture in the wrist. It resembles the curve of the back of a fork.

Jim was in surgery for several hours, and no one came out to tell me how he was. My fear was that he had other maybe life-threatening injuries. Thankfully, neither one of them did. Both boys remained in the hospital for several days. It was certainly a chore bathing and feeding them when they did come home. We got quite a bit of attention out in public.

The boys would tell people, "By golly, we know not to talk back now."

I can only imagine the kind of trouble that would have caused in today's society. Recuperation was long and slow, but they both came through without any permanent damage.

Our four-year tour of duty on Oahu was not up yet when my husband was diagnosed with a blood tumor in his arm and, after extensive surgery, was forced to take a medical discharge. We would be going back to Bremerton. Luckily, our house there was vacant. We all cried to even think of leaving Hawaii. I would be taking many lifelong memories with me. The older boys loved surfing, and we had all become beach bums. I would put my beach cover over my bathing suit and take a huge straw hat and a beach umbrella, and off to the beach we would go. I didn't swim and tried to avoid the sun, so I would find a palm tree to sit under and read while everyone else enjoyed the sand and surf. Now it was all coming to an end. I had made so many friends, watched my children blossom, and come to love this beautiful paradise island.

My friend Ethel had purchased tickets for us to see Elvis at the Honolulu International Center. The concert was taking place the night after the date we had to leave. To top that letdown, it was the middle of December, and none of us had winter coats.

***

Along with all the memories I was taking back to Washington were the wonderful recipes I had gathered during our years on Oahu, one of my favorites being a Hawaiian salad that became my Easter specialty every year.

Hawaiian Salad

1 cup of sugar
2 tablespoons of flour
½ teaspoon of salt
2 eggs, beaten
1 tablespoon of lemon juice
1 ¾ cups of pineapple juice (I use the juice that I drain from the pineapple)

Combine sugar, flour, and salt. Gradually stir in pineapple juice and eggs. Cook over moderate heat, stirring, until thickened. Add lemon juice. Cool mixture to room temperature.

Bring to boil the following:

3 quarts of water
2 teaspoons of salt
1 tablespoon of cooking oil

Add one package (sixteen ounces) of acini di pepe soup pasta. Cook at rolling boil until soup pasta is done (about nine minutes). Drain, rinse with water, drain again, and cool to room temperature.

Combine egg mixture and soup pasta. Mix lightly but thoroughly. Refrigerate overnight in an airtight container.

Add the following:

  3 cans (11 oz. each) of mandarin oranges, drained
  2 cans (20 oz. each) of pineapple chunks, drained
  1 can (20 oz.) of crushed pineapple, drained
  1 carton (8 oz.) of nondairy whipped topping
  1 cup of miniature marshmallows (optional)
  1 cup of coconut (optional)

Mix lightly but thoroughly. Salad may be refrigerated for as long as one week in airtight container. This is a great salad for a potluck or large gathering as it makes twenty-five servings.

***

A hui hou. Until we meet again.

Chapter 5

Returning to our home in Bremerton, Pat's retirement seemed like a positive assurance that life would finally take on a conventional, stable style. This was not to be the case, however. Life doesn't always go as planned or the way we think it should.

It became apparent once we were settled that Pat had no intention of looking for a job. He had been a student most of his military life, the navy paying for all his education. We would not be able to live as well as we had become accustomed on what he would be getting now for disability pay. The only option was for me to go back to work. As luck would have it, I ran into my boss from Sears at the grocery store. I didn't even have to mention a job.

"Hey, when did you get back?" he bellowed across the aisle before I even saw him. Not giving me time to answer, he added, "Your desk is waiting, and I'll have that red phone you wanted for your 'hotline' put in on Monday."

I didn't hesitate to reply, "Okay, I'll see you then."

It was like old home week going back to work. I was able to work the same hours that the kids were in school. Most of the same people were there, and they all seemed happy to have me back. Oh, I also got a raise. Making $5 an hour in 1973 was considered a good wage, as one of my coworkers smirked, "for a woman."

The kids were back in school with their old friends. Maureen had started school in Hawaii, and she was devastated on the first day at her new school when she found out that she had to sit at a desk. They had the "open concept" classrooms in Hawaii, and the kids could sit wherever or nowhere as they chose. She was such a social butterfly and use to flitting around and visiting anyone at will that sitting still and being quiet was foreign to her. She cried the first day because she was scolded several times. Even after explaining the rules to her, she refused to conform. That poor teacher. It took at least two weeks of pleading and threatening before my baby finally adapted. I was afraid she was going to be dispelled from second grade.

Pat decided to use his GI Bill to go to real-estate school. What a great idea—or so I thought. I studied all the books and real-estate laws with him, coached him for his exam, and was thrilled when he got his license. He went to work at a local real-estate office, bought a whole new wardrobe, and left the house smiling every day.

Weeks passed, and whenever I would ask about sales or showing a house, anything job related, I would get a curt reply or no answer at all. I finally quit asking. He was spending long hours at the office, so I figured he was busy, and I would eventually see the rewards for his hard work and dedication. Longer hours away from home, no payday—how long would it take me to figure out that there was something more than real-estate business going on in his life?

When I finally confronted him, he told me that there was a younger gal in his office who played cribbage. I suspected they were playing something other than cards, and after much prodding and questions, he finally admitted that they were having an affair.

My whole world came crashing down around me. I had been with this man, my only love, for half of my life. I remember sitting cross-legged in the middle of the living-room floor with my arms crossed tightly over my chest, rocking back and forth. I knew that my heart was physically breaking. I could feel it. I didn't cry. I couldn't. I couldn't think or speak.

Every woman who is betrayed must wonder, *What did I do or what did I not do to deserve this? How could I not have known?* He left me sitting there, dying inside. He didn't say a word, no apologies, no excuses—he just walked out. That was probably the smart thing to do.

When I finally returned to reality, my first thought was *How can I ever tell the kids?* I decided that I couldn't or wouldn't tell them. Pat was still coming home, acting like everything was fine. I begged him to go to counseling with me, but he refused. He wanted a divorce.

"No" was my immediate reply. "I did not bargain to raise four children alone. You cannot do this to me."

My eldest son, Patrick, who was fifteen, came to me one day and very matter-of-factly told me, "Mother, I cannot stand back and watch you live in this hell. Either he goes or I go." This boy was wiser than his years and much braver than his mother.

When I answered, "I won't let you leave me," he promptly went into my bedroom, got out a suitcase, and began throwing his father's clothes into it. He came out of the room and bluntly asked me, "Are you going to drive me to her house, or do I have to walk?"

He had evidently followed his father to see where he was spending his time, so he knew where to go. We got in the car and crossed the bridge to East Bremerton without even speaking. He got out of the car, walked to the front door, and threw the suitcase. It hit the door with a bang, and his father instantly appeared.

I don't know exactly why I got out of the car, but when Pat saw me walking toward him, he smugly bellowed, "What in the hell are you doing here? Why aren't you at home with your kids, where you belong?"

I don't remember swinging, but I backhanded him hard enough that he was sprawled out on the lawn, mumbling something as Patrick and I drove off.

Many years later, he told me that when he went back into the house, she—Linda was her name—asked him what that was all about, and when he gave her a sarcastic answer, she also knocked him on his ass.

I filed for a divorce, and before it was even finalized, their marriage license announcement was published in the local paper. So like it or not, I was a single working mother. Although child support was ordered, I didn't ever receive a penny until years later when their dad married his third wife. My second son, Don, decided that he wanted to live with his dad, who had moved to Wyoming. I had only thought that my heart was broken up to this point. I could not imagine living without one of my children.

My mother consoled me with her wise words, telling me, "God only gives us our children for a certain time, and it is your time to let Don go."

Being with his dad turned out to be best for both of them.

Now it was time to get on with my life. I knew that I would never, ever trust another man. I stayed busy with the kid's activities and my job, and I immersed myself into cooking. I would read a cookbook as though it were a novel, and I became Julia Child and the Galloping Gourmet's biggest fan. My kids knew that dinner wasn't over until dessert was served. I am sure that if you asked them today what their fondest childhood memory is, it would have something to do with their mama's cooking. I hung a plaque in my kitchen, which read, "Kissin' don't keep. Cookin' do!" How true this was in my case. I found true solace in my culinary fervor.

Other than my work colleagues, the only adults in my life were the boys' Little League coaches and the scout leaders I had met through Cub Scouts. My social life was the Little League concession stand, which I managed. One of the coaches gave me an invitation to attend a Christmas party that he was hosting. He was a naval officer living on base. I was very hesitant to accept the offer, being an ex–navy wife and not knowing most of the people who would be there. I was never shy meeting new people, but I was as nervous as someone getting ready for a first date as I dolled up for my big night out.

As I approached the door and rang the bell, I was beginning to have second thoughts. Too late! The host greeted me graciously and led me down a steep stairway to a sprawling recreation room full of talking, laughing people. I smiled and tried to be sociable as I was introduced to everyone. One quiet, handsome, bearded man who met me at the bottom of the steps was overly attentive, and that made me uneasy. I tried to avoid him in the crowded room, but there he was, watching my every move. He told me much later that when he saw me at the top of the stairs, he announced to everyone in the room that he was going to marry me.

John Richmond Walton III was a relative of Sam Walton, the founder of Walmart. In the 1970s, Walmart was no more than a small retail store in Arkansas. John came from a humble background and a loving, close, religious family. He joined the navy as a young man, married, and had two sons. While he was on deployment, his wife left the very young boys with his parents to babysit while she went shopping. She never returned. His parents took legal custody and raised the boys. John only saw them when he was home on leave, maybe once or twice a year. When I met John, he was preparing to retire after a twenty-year navy career. After spending time with me and the children, he professed his love for us and said that he did not want to go home without us.

Is this man crazy? was my first reaction. *Who in their right mind would want to marry a woman and take on three kids?*

John was wonderful with the kids, and they loved him. I was confused and scared. I could, however, envision a bright future and the security that was lacking in our lives. I knew in my heart that if I refused his offer, I would always wonder, *What if?*

We were married in January 1974 by the navy chaplain at the base chapel. My brother gave me away, and the children were all present.

Oh my god, what have I done? I asked myself almost immediately after the ceremony.

My brother liked John. Everyone who knew him liked him. I didn't even know him. It turned out that his family didn't know him either.

The trip to Missouri was exciting for the kids. Don chose to stay with his dad, which was very hard for me but probably best for him at that time. John's family welcomed all of us with open arms. Patrick was the same age as John's youngest son, Curtis, so he had no problem fitting right in at school. The two younger kids adapted well and loved being a part of the Walton family. The boys enjoyed living near the river, where they fished and speared bullfrogs.

Thomasville is a small town just east of West Plains, Missouri. The house we lived in was originally a theater where Porter Wagoner first introduced Dolly Parton. Across the street from us was the country store/post office.

One day a tourist walked into the store and asked my son Raymond, who was hanging out there with the other boys, "Where's the post office?"

"Right behind the potato chips, ma'am," he replied with a grin.

The neighbors were all congenial, and went out of their way to make us feel welcome. When they plowed our garden space with a horse-drawn plow, the smell of the fresh-turned dirt and the feel of it between my toes gave me a vague inkling that I was going to enjoy country living.

The neighbor up the hill from us milked his cows twice a day, and the local dairy came every morning to pick up the fresh milk. The first spring that I was there, the cows got out of the fence and into a pasture of wild garlic. The dairy couldn't take the milk, of course, so I asked him if I could have it.

"Why?" he asked with a perplexed look on his face.

I had the ingenious idea of taking the cream off the milk, churning it, and making garlic butter. The neighbors were impressed when the new "city girl" distributed it throughout town.

John laughed when I asked for a pig for my birthday. "Most women want jewelry and furs," he said as he gifted me with Nelly.

She was a beauty. When my dad called to wish me a happy birthday, I was excited telling him about my gift.

He chided me, "Nelly, Nelly, with a pigskin belly—put an apple in her mouth, and we'll all have pork and jelly."

As Nelly got bigger, she got a little cantankerous with the kids. I think maybe they teased her. I warned Raymond not to go into the pen when he went to feed Nelly. I was in the yard one evening, hammering a gate onto a post, when I heard a piercing scream coming from the pig pen. Lo and behold, there was Raymond, halfway over the fence, with his right foot firmly engaged in Nelly's mouth. I raced to the fence and raised the hammer, and it came down firmly right between Nelly's eyes. She quickly released him, and as he scurried over the fence, she began staggering in a circle, finally dropping to the ground.

I began screaming hysterically, "I killed Nelly! I killed Nelly!"

The neighbors came running across the yard, not knowing that Nelly was my pig. By this time, she had recovered from the blow enough to get up. The kids were all a little more cautious about going into the pen after that incident.

One of the neighbors, hearing how much I loved my pig, brought me a runt black-and-white Hampshire piglet who had been rejected by its mother. I took it upon myself to feed it with a doll bottle every two hours. We named her Li'l Bit and kept her in a box in the kitchen.

One day the local dentist's wife, who thought that she was better than us common folk, came to the house with my mother-in-law. When she saw the piglet under the kitchen table, she snootily inquired, "Isn't that a little unsanitary?"

"Oh, the pig doesn't seem to mind," I acknowledged with a smile.

I raised a big red Hampshire pig for another neighbor. We couldn't keep him in the pen with the other pigs because he was lame, and they picked on him, so he became our yard pet. The kids rode him and toted him around on a leash. The owner eventually came to take Big Red to the butcher. We didn't tell Maureen where he was going. The boys, being boys, waited to tell her when I served ground pork sausage. She doesn't eat ground sausage to this day without thinking of Big Red.

The first time the boys came home with a huge burlap sack full of freshly speared bullfrogs, I was reluctant to even peek in the bag.

"Let's cook them now!" Curtis was squealing, eyes glowing and licking his lips.

I was staring at these ugly, slimy creatures, trying to imagine how or why anyone would want to cook them.

"Just the legs, Mom, just the legs," Patrick chimed in when he realized that I was visualizing the whole frog. "You've heard of eating frogs legs? It's a delicacy," he added in an excited tone of voice.

"It is ten o'clock at night, and you want me to cook frog's legs?" I was actually amused to see these boys so excited over their big kill. "I don't even want to touch them, let alone clean them," I said without hesitation.

"We'll butcher them and clean them" was their quick reply as they scurried out the back door.

"Be sure and skin them."

They ran to show the neighbor, who was more than willing to help them with the cleaning, but who was going to help me with the chore of cooking them?

"Oh, just fry them like you would chicken," the neighbor's wife advised me.

Okay, I'm ready for this. Fry pan, cooking oil, flour, salt, and pepper.

She forgot to mention to me that after you wash and salt them and put them in the hot oil, they begin to dance. The kids thought this was really funny, but it freaked me out.

Our midnight snack turned out to be a delightful event, which we repeated every couple of months with most of the neighbors participating. Frog's legs are the only thing that come out of the water that I will eat, and I love them. No, they do not taste like chicken.

As my friend Bob said recently, "They taste like frog's legs."

The texture is something of a cross between fish and chicken, but they have a taste all their own. You don't have to kiss a frog to succumb to the succulent flavor.

***

Simple Sautéed Frog's Legs

Soak legs in milk for one hour, turning every fifteen minutes. Remove from milk and salt and pepper lightly and then coat in flour. Bring butter or oil to a sizzle and add frog's legs. Sauté uncovered until they are golden brown, turning as needed. You can also dip them into an egg/milk mixture and coat with a cracker or cornflake mixture and fry in hot oil. The last time I cooked them, I ate twelve.

Is a mother ever ready for her son's first girlfriend? Patrick met Diane on his first day at his new school. The name of Diane's mother was Ruby, and from day one, I heard more about Ruby than I heard about her daughter. The kids all loved Ruby, and I could hardly wait to meet her.

"Wait till you taste her Ruby Burger, Mom."

I finally met her at a baseball game, and I think the very first words out of my mouth after being introduced were "How do you make a Ruby Burger?"

She and everyone around us laughed. Evidently, that was her claim to fame.

"Ground beef and a bun" Was her quick, dry answer. Then with a little grin and a wink, she gave up her secret.

***

Ruby Burgers

Select top-grade ground beef. Sprinkle with seasoned salt. Use about one third of a pound of meat per patty. Brown on one side on flat grill. Flip and place one slice of American cheese on browned side. Place the bottom of an onion bun on top of cheese, top of the bun on top. Cover and cook slowly so that the cheese will melt and bun will steam. Serve with mustard, pickle, and onion.

That's it! Simple. Just a plain ol' burger, made special by a special lady.

***

To this day, the only burger we serve at our house is the Ruby Burger. I believe that the onion bun and steaming it on the meat is the secret. I have some of Ruby's favorite recipes written on scraps of paper, coasters, and the backs of baseball programs, whatever was available to write on when we started talking food. Thanks, Ruby, for all the wonderful memories you have given us. Following are a few more of the best of Ruby's best recipes.

Ruby's Oatmeal Pie

Tastes just like pecan pie.

2 eggs
⅔ cup of melted butter
⅔ cup of sugar
⅔ cup of light corn syrup
¼ teaspoon of salt
⅔ cup of uncooked oatmeal (regular or quick-cooking)
1 teaspoon of vanilla
1 unbaked eight-inch pie shell

Mix ingredients together and pour into uncooked pie shell. Bake at 350 degrees about one hour.

Ruby's Oatmeal Cake

1 cup of oatmeal	1 ½ cups of boiling water
1 cup of white sugar	1 cup of brown sugar
½ cup of shortening	2 eggs

Mix and add the following:

1 ⅓ cup of flour	1 teaspoon of cinnamon
½ teaspoon of baking soda	1 teaspoon of salt

Bake in nine-by-thirteen-by-two-inch pan at 350 degrees for forty-five minutes.

Icing for Oatmeal Cake

¼ cup of cream   ¼ cup of butter
½ cup of brown sugar

Bring mixture to a boil. Remove from heat and add the following:

1 cup of coconut   ½ cup of chopped nuts

Frost the cake and then put under broiler until brown.

Doctor Bud Cake

Mix well in a large bowl.

3 cups of flour   2 cups of sugar
1 teaspoon of baking soda   1 teaspoon salt
1 teaspoon of cinnamon

Add the following:

1 ½ cups of cooking oil
3 slightly beaten eggs
½ cup of chopped nuts
2 cups of diced bananas (very ripe)
1 8 oz. can of crushed pineapple
1 ½ teaspoon of vanilla

Mix well by hand. Do not use mixer. Bake in tube pan at 350 degrees for one hour and twenty minutes.

Marinated Carrot Salad

2 pounds of carrots, sliced, cooked to barely tender (still firm), drained, and cooled
1 medium onion, sliced thin
1 green pepper, sliced thin

Mix the following:

1 can of tomato soup, undiluted
½ cup of oil
½ cup of sugar
½ cup of cider vinegar
½ teaspoon of Worcestershire sauce
½ teaspoon of pepper

Bring to a boil and then cool. In casserole dish, layer carrots and onions. Pour marinade over and then add green pepper slices. Refrigerate (at least overnight) in airtight container.

***

The Watergate Scandal began in June 1972 when five men were arrested for breaking and entering into the DNC headquarters at the Watergate Complex in Washington, D.C. The FBI investigated and discovered a slush fund used by the Nixon campaign. They also revealed a wire-tapping system in the president's office. The Supreme Court ruled that President Nixon had to release any tape-recorded conversations. He denied that he was aware of any wrongdoing. Facing impeachment and probably conviction for his cover-up of political scandals and illegal activities, Nixon resigned in August 1974.

The whole nation was abuzz about Watergate. It was at this time that I started working part-time at the Sears Service Center in West Plains. There were three other women in the office, and their only goal ever was to outdo one another in the cooking arena. So when one of them showed up with her Watergate salad, one of the others had to top it the next day with her Watergate cake. I didn't comprehend the connection of pistachio nuts and politics, but both the dishes were scrumptious.

***

Watergate Salad

1 8 oz. container of Cool Whip
1 box of instant pistachio pudding
1 20 oz. can crushed pineapple, with juice
1 cup of miniature marshmallows
½ cup of chopped walnuts

Mix all ingredients and refrigerate. Quick, easy, and *good*.

Watergate Cake

1 white cake mix
¾ cup of oil
3 eggs
1 cup of 7 Up or club soda
1 package (3 oz.) of pistachio instant pudding
1 cup of chopped pecans
½ cup of coconut

Combine cake mix, oil, eggs, and soda; mix well. Stir in pudding, pecans, and coconut. Pour into a greased and floured nine-by-thirteen-inch pan. Bake at 350 degrees for forty-five minutes.

Cover-Up Icing

2 envelopes (3 oz. each) of Dream Whip (dry topping mix)
1 ½ cups milk (or one 8 oz. container of Cool Whip)
1 package (3 oz.) of pistachio instant pudding
½ cup of coconut
¾ cup of chopped pecans

Combine topping mix, milk, and pudding (or Cool Whip and pudding). Beat until thick. Spread on cake and sprinkle with coconut and pecans.

***

The church in Thomasville was Baptist, and being raised Catholic, I was not comfortable attending their services. When I started work in West Plains, it was convenient for me to attend Saturday evening mass at the church there when I got off work. As I was driving home after mass one fall evening, I spotted a deer on the side of the road about fifty feet ahead. It was already dusk and raining profusely. It crossed my mind at that moment that this was opening day of hunting season. The guys at work had all been talking about their weekend plans.

I slowed down as I got close enough to see Bambi's eyes in my headlights, and just as I thought I had passed him, he jumped on the hood of my car. He bounced off into the other lane. He was still moving, but I was afraid to get out of the car. I was only about five miles to my turnoff, so I continued on, crying like a baby.

When I walked into the house, my son, just looking at me, knew that something was wrong. "Are you all right, Mother?"

"No, I just hit a deer."

"But are *you* all right?"

He calmed me down, and I called the state patrol to report the deer on the road.

"We can't pick it up tonight, ma'am. Can you use the meat?"

Patrick called our neighbor Bob, and they went and loaded the deer into the truck, took it to Bob's barn, and hung it. I couldn't bear to look at it, let alone ever consider eating it. When Bob delivered the meat to us, all butchered, wrapped, and frozen, a few days later, I had second thoughts, however. John's friend Don said that he would not eat wild meat, even if it had been killed legally.

The first thing I did when I got back to work Monday morning was show off my Polaroid photo of the deer hanging and inquired if anyone else had gotten their deer. I think that it was the best venison I have ever eaten. Don happened to be at the house one day when I had a big pot of my "best ever stew" simmering and biscuits in the oven.

"Sure smells good in here," he commented.

"Well, you are welcome to stay and have dinner with us."

I knew that he would accept the offer.

"That was the best beef stew I have ever eaten," he complimented me after dinner with a huge grin and a big hug.

"That was my roadkill, Don." I laughed.

***

Best Ever Beef Stew

3 tablespoons of olive oil

2 pounds of cubed stew beef (or venison)

1 medium onion, diced

3 cloves of garlic, minced

12 ounces of beer (pale lager)

3 ½ cups of beef broth

2 tablespoons of tomato paste

1 tablespoon of Worcestershire sauce

1 ½ teaspoons of sugar

½ teaspoon of paprika

8 new potatoes, quartered

4 carrots, sliced diagonally

3 tablespoons of flour

Brown seasoned meat for six minutes. Remove. Add onion and cook, stirring on low heat for three minutes. Add garlic and cook for one minute. Pour in beer. Add broth and tomato paste, Worcestershire, sugar, paprika, and half a teaspoon of kosher salt and pepper to taste. Return meat and simmer for one and a half to two hours. Stir in potatoes and carrots. Simmer for thirty- to forty minutes until tender. Remove one cup of liquid, whisk in flour, and stir. Add to stew. Bring to a boil and simmer for ten minutes.

***

Don, the very same fellow who said he wouldn't eat wild meat, showed up at my door one Sunday with a bucket full of something I was very unsure of.

"How 'bout fryin' these up for me?" he asked with a grin.

"What is it?" I inquired.

"Rocky Mountain oysters. You're a Montana girl. You should be familiar with these."

He had just castrated his calves and saved the "golden nuggets" for me. I laughed, remembering the annual Testicle Festival every year in Montana. I had never tried them, but cooking them couldn't be any worse than frying frog's legs. I was game.

We washed them, and he skinned them. I dipped them in egg and milk, shook them in crushed cracker crumbs, deep-fried them, and served them for dinner. The kids were gobbling them up and asking for more until Don told them what they were eating!

I was quite amused as I shared the jingle they used at the festival in Montana—"Come on down and have a ball!"

On the days that I worked, my mother-in-law, Lorene, insisted that I have lunch with her. She was a delightful lady, so I was happy to accept her offer. I had an hour for lunch, and she lived just five minutes from the store. She seemed to take great pleasure in fixing my lunch, and I thought it was a good opportunity to get to know her and hear stories of John and his sister's childhood. That didn't turn out to be the case, however.

"This is Macdonald Carey, and these are the days of our lives" would greet me as I walked through the front door, and I was only allowed to talk during the commercials. So most days, I would just sit quietly and eat. When she did talk, she loved sharing her recipes with me and usually had a good story to go with each one of them. Her grandmother Sanders was born in 1850 and passed down many stories about the Civil War and the James brothers. Jesse James and his brother Frank came from the Little Dixie area of Western Missouri, the same territory as the Sanders family. Jesse joined the Confederate army at age sixteen. After his military service, he became a notorious outlaw and was assassinated at age thirty-four by one of his cohorts, Robert Ford, in 1882. Lorene claimed that Grandma Sanders depicted the James brothers as "good boys" who loved oatmeal cookies. You have only to look at my recipe card, written in Lorene's handwriting, to know that these were and still are the most popular cookies in our house.

***

Grandma Sanders's Oatmeal Cookies

1 cup of brown sugar (packed)   1 cup of butter
2 eggs   1 cup of regular oatmeal
2 cups of flour   1 teaspoon of baking soda
1 teaspoon of cloves   1 teaspoon of cinnamon
1 cup of chopped dates or raisins 1 cup of chopped nuts
¼ cup of milk

Cream brown sugar and butter; add eggs. Combine dry ingredients and oatmeal. Add to sugar mixture alternately with milk. Stir in dates or raisins and nuts. Drop by teaspoon, about one inch apart, on lightly greased cookie sheet. Bake in 350-degree oven for ten to twelve minutes or until lightly browned.

***

Lorene's friend Emma made this luscious mandarin orange salad for our lunch one day, and when I asked for the recipe, she just blurted it out without hesitation. I guess she had made it often enough that she didn't need a written copy. It is quick and delish.

Mandarin Orange Salad

1 small (8 oz.) container of Cool Whip
1 can (11 oz.) of mandarin oranges, drained and diced
1 small (8 oz.) can of crushed pineapple, also drained
1 box (4 oz.) of orange Jell-O (dry)
½ cup of cottage cheese
½ cup of sour cream

Sprinkle Jell-O over and fold into Cool Whip mixture. Chill.

***

Blanch was the "Aunt Bea" of Thomasville. She lived all her life in the huge old two-story house with the god-awful flowered wallpaper covering most of the walls. I don't know if she was a widow or had never been married. She loved to cook and never, ever made just enough for herself, so we were treated often to her leftovers. When I would see her come to the door, bearing gifts, and inquire as to what she had for us, her answer was always the same—"Mus'-goes" (translated—"I cooked this yesterday and couldn't eat it all, so it *must go* today.") My very favorite of her creations was this oven chow mein.

Oven Chow Mein

1½ pounds of ground beef (you can use half pork)
2 tablespoons butter.

Lightly brown beef in butter. Add the following:

2 cups of chopped celery	2 cups of chopped onions
1 cup of uncooked rice	2 cups of hot water
1 can of cream-of-mushroom soup	⅓ cup of soy sauce
½ teaspoon of salt	¼ teaspoon of pepper

Cover and bake at 350 degrees for one hour. Stir while baking.

***

Every Saturday night, the boys and their friends would gather at our house to watch *Saturday Night Live*. I would pop popcorn, and someone would provide sodas. It was nice knowing where the kids were. My son brought home recipes from Ruby for caramel corn and peanut butter fudge, hoping that I would agree to try them for Saturday-night treats. I did, of course.

Never-Fail Peanut Butter Fudge

2 cups of sugar
2 tablespoons of butter
Dash of salt

1 cup of milk
¾ cup of peanut butter, smooth or crunchy
1 teaspoon of vanilla

Boil sugar, milk, and salt for ten minutes. Add butter. Continue boiling until mixture forms a soft ball in cold water. Remove from heat; add vanilla and peanut butter. Beat until mixture starts to set. Pour quickly into buttered pan. Cool and cut into squares.

Caramel Popcorn

Use three quarts of popped popcorn. Measure into saucepan one cup of sugar. Stir over low heat until melted and golden brown.

Stir in carefully the following:

¾ cup of hot water
½ cup of brown sugar

Cook at 238 degrees or until a little of the mixture forms a soft ball when dropped into cold water. Pour over popped corn. Mix gently to coat well. Press into balls or spread out to cool so that pieces separate.

***

Our first Christmas in Missouri could have been taken directly from a movie. It was picture-perfect. Grandpa Walton played the piano, and the family all gathered around and sang hymns and Christmas carols. My new family was so impressed with my cookie baking. Besides all my regular Christmas cookies, I added two new recipes that year.

Peppermint Candy Cookies Surprise

Make the recipe for Mexican wedding cakes.

Filling and Rolling Mixture

Combine half a cup of crushed peppermint candy with half a cup of powdered sugar (sifted). Set aside. Cream together two tablespoons of cream cheese and one teaspoon of milk.

Add very gradually the following:

½ cup confectioners' sugar
1 drop of red food coloring
3 tablespoons of peppermint candy mix from above (reserving remainder for rolling cookies in)

Mix well. Fill Mexican wedding cakes by poking small holes in the center and placing filling and then reroll cookies. Bake at 350 degrees for twelve to fifteen minutes. While still warm, roll in reserved peppermint candy/sugar mixture. Roll again when cool.

Holiday Cherry Squares

1 ½ cups of cornflake crumbs
½ cup butter, softened
3 tablespoons of sugar
2 cups of miniature marshmallows
1 ⅓ cups of flaked coconut
1 10 oz. jar of chopped Maraschino cherries
1 (14 oz.) can of sweetened condensed milk
1 cup of chopped nuts

In a thirteen-by-nine-by-two-inch baking pan, combine cornflake crumbs, butter, and sugar. Press down firmly with back of spoon.

Sprinkle marshmallows, coconut, and cherries evenly over crumb crust. Pour sweetened condensed milk evenly over top. Sprinkle nuts evenly over condensed milk, pressing lightly into mixture. Bake at 350 degrees about twenty-five minutes or until lightly browned around edges. Refrigerate before cutting.

As the new year approached, I began to notice changes in John's behavior. How could I have not realized up until now that he had a drinking problem? Even his parents were not aware of his alcoholism. He was never mean, never abusive, verbally or physically, just sometimes very quiet and distant. This moodiness began to wear on me as my main goal in life was to make this man happy.

He had given me a beautiful new car for Christmas. I was surprised and very grateful as I had never had a brand new car.

I was washing it one day, and he approached me and said, "I think that you love that car more than you love me."

Being quite flippant, I replied, "You might just be right."

He grabbed the keys, and away he drove. I shrugged it off, went in the house, and started dinner, knowing that he would be right back.

It's funny how we associate food with happenings in our lives. I remember clearly that I was cooking one of John's favorite dinners, pork chops and rice.

Pork-Chop Rice Casserole

In hot oil, brown six to eight– lean center-cut pork chops. Place in baking dish or Dutch oven. Put one slice of onion and one slice of green pepper on each chop. Sprinkle three quarters of a cup of uncooked rice over chops. Add two (twenty-ounce) cans of chopped tomatoes (I use the Italian-flavored variety). Salt and pepper to taste.

Cover and bake in 350-degree oven for one and a half hours. Delicious served with baked summer squash.

***

An hour passed, and I began to wonder why John wasn't back. There was a knock at the door.

"Mrs. Walton?" questioned the tall uniformed man facing me.

"Yes?" I replied in a tremulous voice.

"Your car is on the bottom of the Eleven Point River."

"And John?" I questioned.

"Oh he's okay. We took him in on a DUI."

This was just the beginning of my year of hell. His behavior became more and more erratic, and I was beginning to be very uncomfortable around him and concerned for my kids. He had always been good with the kids, and I didn't want them to witness his volatile outbursts.

One day my shoes were sitting on the fireplace mantle, and for no apparent reason, John threw them into the fire. I had given him a sheepskin-lined denim jacket for Christmas. He threw it into the fire. He threw his sound-system speakers into the fire. These actions were not done in fits of rage or drunkenness; they were just random acts of crazy. I knew that my perfect dream life was turning into a nightmare and that my only option was to leave before it escalated.

I should have known but evidently didn't that you never, ever try to reason with a drunk. He had been drinking the night that I told him that I was planning to leave. He laughed and told me that I could never leave him. I guess to prove his point, he went into the bedroom and came out with his gun. He started to cry and told me that he felt sorry for me. It was eleven o'clock, and the kids had been in bed for hours. I quickly woke them while he was ranting and raving and told them to get in the car immediately. If he was going to shoot me, I wanted to be sure that the kids were out of the house. I grabbed my purse and ran to the car with my daughter in tow. I literally threw her in the back seat and slammed the door with her nightgown caught in it. I heard the bullets as I screeched out of the driveway.

I drove ninety miles an hour to West Plains, about thirty miles away. I prayed that he wasn't following me. I drove directly to the police station, but of course, there was no one there at midnight. I had no choice but to go to his parents' house. They listened to my story in shock.

"I don't know what has gotten into John. He was perfectly normal until he met you," his mother informed me.

I guess I was right. They didn't know him.

John's father took me back to the house the next day to collect my personal belongings. I did not even look at John, and we didn't speak. The seven bullet holes in the car told the story clearly. I knew that I had not failed but still felt ashamed and embarrassed to face my family. I wanted to just erase this whole chapter of my life and pretend that it never happened.

My mom and dad were visiting my sister in Fallon, Nevada, so I headed straight there. I spent days explaining all that had ensued to my family and somehow trying to justify my leaving. They were understanding, comforted me, and assured me that I had done the right thing.

On the Saturday evening after I arrived, my mother wanted to go to mass. My dad and I were going to go with her, but on the way there, we decided to drop her off at church and spend the hour waiting for her at the Nugget Casino. Playing the nickel slot machines with my dad was the most fun I had had in a long time. We picked Mother up on time, and when we got back to my sister's house, she announced to me that John Walton had called her.

"Of course, I told him you were not here. You weren't," she assured me.

When I asked her where he had called from, my heart skipped a beat when she said, "The Nugget."

He had followed me to Nevada. He knew that my sister lived in Fallon, but thankfully, he didn't have her address. I guess he gave up when she said that I wasn't there. I never saw him again.

I was relieved when I received divorce papers in the mail when I got back to Washington. I read the decree and tucked it carefully into a drawer. It wasn't until years later that I learned that the papers I had received were a summons for me to appear in court before the divorce could be finalized.

The nightmare was over, but it was years before I could talk about it. When I left Missouri, I promised myself that I would never look back. John has since passed away, and now I smile, remembering and sharing with my children stories of the good times, good friends, and good food that we experienced in Missouri, memories that I now cherish as a special time of my life.

Chapter 6

Leaving my failed marriage behind, I returned to Washington State. My two youngest children were teenagers at the time. They would be able to continue school in the state that we considered home. I promised them that his would be our last move after years of military life and new schools every few years. I was certain that I could go back to work for Sears. I had worked for them for eleven years in three states.

We settled in a quaint little logging area on Highway 2, about half an hour east of Everett. Gold Bar seemed like the perfect place for the kids to thrive. They adapted well and soon had new friends and were anxious to start school in nearby Sultan. The nearest service department hiring for Sears was in South Seattle, at least an hour away, up to three hours in prime-time traffic. My brother thought that it would be a great idea for us to move to Seattle to be near him and his family, but I had given the kids my word that we were not going to move again. I knew there must be a local retail or grocery-store clerk job available in the area. I enjoyed working with people, so that would be an option.

On the day the kids started school, my new neighbor, Lisa, invited me to have lunch with her. Her friends owned a restaurant, the Chuckwagon, on the main street of Sultan. The owners greeted us at the door, and Lisa introduced me to them. She promptly told them that I was looking for a job. Bob's eyes lit up, and he quickly informed me that they were in the process of adding a bar.

"Do you know how to tend bar?" he inquired.

"Well, uh, I did cocktail-waitress for my dad once at a wedding" was my lame reply. I had no idea on earth how to mix a drink, but I figured that I could open a beer, and what do loggers drink?

By the end of lunch, I had agreed to take the job until I could find something permanent. I was offered $3.50 an hour plus tips. They were still in the process of completing the addition for the bar, but they said that I could start the next day. My first duties as the new bar manager were to order all the glassware, contact the vendors for supplies and delivery schedules, and write up the liquor order. I had no idea whatsoever what I was getting into.

"Oh well, it's only a part-time job. I can handle it," I assured my brother when he questioned my decision to take the job.

Within a week, the owners, Bob and LeMoine, had me feeling like one of the family. I checked out *Old Mr. Boston's Bartender's Guide* and learned the difference between a highball glass and a brandy snifter. I wanted to go to the other local bar to check out what kind of liquor they served, but I wouldn't have dreamed of walking into a bar alone, and I had no one to take me, so I just roamed the local liquor store and scoped out what I thought we would need. I also learned that vodka and orange juice was not a "screw ball."

Bob hired an older experienced bartender, Peggy. She was more than happy to teach me the art of mixology. She had been tending bar for several years and was a letter-perfect example of Carla, the bartender from the TV sitcom *Cheers*. She had an answer for everything and knew her booze well.

My first customer questioned me, "What is your bar whiskey?"

"Ten High," I replied, feeling quite smug about my choice of spirits.

"Oh no, I want a good blended whiskey."

Peggy had neglected to teach me the difference between a bourbon and a blended whiskey, so I smiled, put a shot of Ten High in the blender, blended it, and served it to him. The poor guy almost fell off the barstool laughing.

That was just the beginning of my bartending career. The bets were on—I wouldn't last three weeks.

Peggy had her own index box of bar recipes. From her, I learned to make the best hot-buttered-rum batter and Tom and Jerry mix ever, formulas that I have passed on to many others over the years.

***

Hot Buttered Rum Mix

2 pounds of brown sugar   1 pound of butter
1 pint of vanilla ice cream

Mix and freeze.

Tom and Jerry Mix

6 egg yolks   ¼ teaspoon of cream of tartar
1 pound of brown sugar   6 egg whites
1 pound of powdered sugar

Stir together egg yolks, brown sugar, and cream of tartar. Beat egg whites until stiff. Add powdered sugar and fold gently into egg mixture.

***

At Christmastime, Peggy would make bourbon balls that even nondrinkers could get a buzz from. I make them with rum instead of bourbon. They are luscious either way.

Bourbon or Rum Balls

2 ½ cups of finely crushed vanilla wafers 1 cup of powdered sugar
1 cup of coarsely chopped nuts 2 tablespoons of cocoa
3 tablespoons of light corn syrup ¼ cup of bourbon or rum

Mix well. Shape into balls. Roll in powdered sugar. Keep in airtight container.

***

Some of her other "magic potions," as she called them, were her homemade Tia Maria, Kahlúa, and Irish cream.

Tia Maria

2 cups of water 1 vanilla bean
4 cups of sugar 2 cups of brandy
2 ounces of instant coffee 2 cups of vodka

Mix water, sugar, and coffee. Bring to a boil. Remove from heat. Cut up vanilla bean (cut bean in half lengthwise and then in pieces). Put in a gallon jug. Pour in hot mixture. When cool, add brandy. Let sit for thirty days and then add vodka.

Kahlúa

4 cups of water 4 cups of sugar
2 ounces of instant coffee 2 vanilla beans (split lengthwise)

Boil water and sugar until dissolved. Remove from heat and add instant coffee. Let cool. Pour into large jar or bottle. Add vanilla beans and one fifth of cheap whiskey. Age for two weeks.

Quick Kahlúa

1 ½ cups water   2 cups sugar
⅓ cup of instant coffee

Mix and bring to boil. Cool to room temperature in refrigerator. Add one teaspoon of vanilla and one or two cups of vodka.

***

My first Christmas at the bar, I made Peggy's Irish cream for some of my customers, who were, in fact, the only friends I had. I gave them as gifts with a little poem that I wrote.

Hi, I'm Baileys "Let's Pretend,"
A creamy, chocolate Irish blend,
A holiday gift of joy and cheer
To share throughout the coming year.
With coffee, I'm a natural.
With brandy, or alone . . .
And here's the magic formula
To mix me up at home.

***

Baileys "Let's Pretend"

1 cup Irish whiskey (I prefer a Canadian blend)
1 cup of half-and-half or whipping cream
3 eggs
1 can of sweetened condensed milk
1 tablespoon of chocolate syrup

Mix in blender. Keep refrigerated. Shake well before serving.

***

While going through my bar recipes, I came across a well-used index card, on which was written, "Compliments of Carroll Lee Johnson." Lee, wherever you are, I share your splendiferous potion with anyone who is brave enough to try it.

Tiki-Tiki Punch

1 part gin

1 part dark rum

2 parts whiskey

4 parts orange juice

2 parts light rum

2 parts one-hundred-proof vodka

4 parts pineapple juice

Add more juice if necessary. Chill.

This punch is so tasty that you don't realize how potent it is. Drink with care.

Note from Lee: *"Real cool, man."*

***

Peggy was not only an extraordinary bartender; she was also a marvelous cook who wooed her customers with her delectable desserts.

Peggy's Perfect Peach Pie

In an unbaked nine-inch pie shell, slice seven peaches. Mix together and pour over peaches:

1 cup of sugar

1 teaspoon of vanilla

½ cup of whipping cream

½ teaspoon of salt

2 tablespoons of cornstarch

Top with slivered almonds. Bake at four hundred degrees for fifteen minutes. Reduce heat to 350 degrees and bake for an additional forty minutes.

Note: I brush the unbaked crust with beaten egg white to keep it from getting soggy.

***

Another of Peggy's well-loved pies became my daughter's choice for her birthday every year.

Peanut Butter Pie

1 cup of creamy peanut butter
1 8 oz. package of cream cheese
1 cup of sugar
2 tablespoons of melted butter
1 cup of whipping cream or Cool Whip
1 tablespoon of vanilla

Mix and place in eight-inch chocolate cookie crust. Chill for six to eight hours. Top with fudge sundae sauce. Chill again for thirty minutes.

***

If you find yourself with no eggs and wanting to bake something special, this pumpkin bread is one of the recipes that Ms. Peggy gave me that I use every year for Thanksgiving.

Pumpkin Bread

3 cups of sugar

2 cups of canned pumpkin

1 cup of oil

2 teaspoons of baking soda

1 teaspoon of nutmeg

3 ⅓ cups of flour

1 ½ teaspoons of salt

⅔ cup of water

1 teaspoon of cinnamon

1 teaspoon of vanilla

Add nuts if desired.

Bake at 350 degrees for about an hour. Makes four small loaves or one angel food pan and one loaf.

***

When Bob and LeMoine sold the Chuckwagon, Les and Ada McCombs, who owned the Sportsman's Inn, asked me if I would be interested in managing their bar. They offered me a considerable raise in pay. Wow! By this time, I knew a little more about the bar business and also knew almost everyone in town.

I think it is common knowledge that a bartender has to be counselor, priest, advisor, part mom, and part cop. In my case, I also became the local logger's banker. This came about quite accidently one day when an unemployed logger came to me upset because he had been offered a job but did not have $40 for the cork boots that were required to work in the woods. I took the check that I had just written for my utility bill out of the envelope, cashed it, and gave him $40.

Much to my dismay, as soon as he left the bar smiling, his sister, Sherry, who worked in the restaurant, came into the bar and said to me, "I sure hope you didn't give Gary money. You'll never get it back."

Friday was payday, and Gary returned, as he had promised, and handed me $50. When I tried to give him $10 back, he refused it, saying that it was my tip for helping him out. I thanked him and put the $10 in an envelope with his name on it in a drawer in my office. By the end of that year, I had a boot box full of envelopes with seven or eight different names, all of whom were borrowing their own money from me and tipping me generously. They would borrow $10 or $20 during the week and pay me back, sometimes even double. I was also getting 20 percent of anything I collected on returned checks from my boss, so I had my own little bank business.

One of the first bartenders I hired was a tall good-looking young man named Ron. He would be my part-time fill-in help. Ron was raised by mute parents, so he was naturally very soft-spoken. He had a beautiful singing voice, and even though it was long before the karaoke era, he and I would sing along together to the jukebox. The Carpenters and Rod Stewart were our favorites.

One day he approached me to sing with him at a wedding. "We've Only Just Begun" was the requested tune.

I responded with a laugh. "My 'singing in the shower' voice is certainly not something to be flaunted in public."

He was disappointed but accepted my gracious refusal.

Ron was a farrier by trade and worked for a local rancher. Being a bachelor, he was always thrilled when someone brought him homemade goodies. One day he surprised us with brownies. He was so proud that he made them himself. They were a big hit with our regular customers, as were all the zucchini breads he learned to make in the summer when his garden flourished.

***

Ron's Brownie Points

½ pound of butter
¾ cup of granulated sugar
¾ cup of brown sugar
2 eggs

1 tablespoon of Kahlúa
1 tablespoon of vanilla
1 ½ cups of white flour
Dash of salt
½ teaspoon of baking soda
½ cup of roasted hazelnuts, chopped
½ cup pecans, chopped
½ cup of walnuts, chopped
½ cup semisweet chocolate chips
1 tablespoon of French dark roasted instant coffee
4 ounces of dark unsweetened baking chocolate, melted

Cream butter and sugars at low speed. Add eggs, coffee, Kahlúa, and vanilla. Mix in melted chocolate. Combine flour, salt, and soda; add to mixture, being careful not to overmix. Fold in nuts and chocolate chips. Grease nine-by-eleven-inch pan. Bake at 350 degrees for about fifteen minutes. Brownies will appear to be undercooked but will continue to cook for about twenty minutes after removed from oven.

I was a little dubious about trying this recipe, but it turns out yummy every time—rich, gooey, nutty, and delicious.

***

Zesty Zucchini Bread

1 cup of sugar

2 eggs

½ teaspoon of grated lemon peel

2 teaspoon of baking powder

½ teaspoon of salt

1 cup of shredded zucchini

½ cup of oil

1 ½ cups of flour

½ teaspoon of orange peel

½ teaspoon of baking soda

¼ teaspoon of allspice

½ cup of chopped nuts

Beat together sugar, oil, eggs, and lemon and orange peels. Add sifted dry ingredients alternately with shredded zucchini. Beat well. Add nuts. Pour into a greased nine-by-five-inch loaf pan. Bake in preheated 350-degree oven for fifty-five minutes. Cool in pan for fifteen minutes.

Ron's Favorite Zucchini Bread

3 eggs

2 cups of sugar

3 cups of flour

1 teaspoon of baking soda

2 teaspoons of cinnamon

¾ cup of chopped nuts

1 cup of oil

2 cups of shredded zucchini

1 teaspoon of salt

¼ teaspoon of baking powder

1 teaspoon of vanilla

Beat eggs until light and foamy. Add oil, sugar, zucchini, and vanilla. Mix lightly but well.

Add sifted dry ingredients; mix and blend. Add nuts. Pour batter into two greased nine-by-five-inch pans. Bake in 350-degree oven for one hour or until done. Cool on rack ten minutes.

Pineapple Zucchini Bread

Using the recipe for Ron's favorite zucchini bread, add one small can (eight and a quarter ounces) of crushed pineapple (drained). Increase baking soda to two teaspoons and baking powder to half a teaspoon. Add one cup of raisins if desired.

***

There must have been a bumper crop of zucchini that year because every day someone brought us a treat made from the fruits of their labor. Well, in this case, it was the vegetable from their garden.

Orange Zucchini Squares

1 cup of sugar	1 ½ cups of flour
1 teaspoon of baking soda	½ teaspoon of salt
1 teaspoon of cinnamon	1 teaspoon of baking powder
1 cup of grated zucchini	½ cup of nuts
2 egg of whites	½ cup of thawed orange juice concentrate
4 tablespoons of vegetable oil	1 ½ teaspoons of orange peel

Mix dry ingredients together. Stir in nuts and zucchini. Beat egg whites and add the orange juice and oil. Fold into dry ingredients. Add orange peel. Spoon into greased and floured nine-by-thirteen-inch pan. Bake at 350 degrees for forty to forty-five minutes.

Chocolate Zucchini Cake

½ cup of butter (softened)	½ cup of vegetable oil
1 ¾ cups of sugar	1 teaspoon of vanilla
½ cup of sour milk	4 tablespoons of cocoa
½ teaspoon of baking powder	½ teaspoon of cloves
2 cups of finely chopped zucchini	¼ cup of chocolate chips
2 ½ cups of flour	

Cream butter, oil, sugar, vanilla, eggs, and sour milk. Beat well. Add sifted dry ingredients. Mix well. Add chocolate chips (and nuts if desired). Bake at 350 degrees in two nine-inch pans or one nine-by-thirteen-inch pan for forty minutes.

***

Ron loved cheesecake. He told me that was all he wanted for his birthday. Oh no, I had never even attempted to make a cheesecake. Caleen, one of the waitresses who worked in the restaurant, came to my rescue and saved the day when she made her much-touted blueberry cream cheese squares. They turned out to be a favorite treat for everyone who was lucky enough to try them, and Ron was in hog heaven. I did learn to make cheesecake in time for his next birthday.

Blueberry Cream Cheese Squares

¼ cup of cornstarch
½ cup of sugar
½ cup of water
3 cups of blueberries
1 ½ sticks of butter, melted
2 8 oz. packs of cream cheese, softened
1 ½ cups of sugar
2 teaspoons of vanilla
1 8 oz. carton of frozen whipped topping
1 package (13 ½ oz.) of graham cracker crumbs

Mix cornstarch, sugar, water, and blueberries and cook, stirring constantly until sauce bubbles and thickens. Cool. Combine cracker crumbs and butter. Press crumbs into a nine-by-thirteen-inch pan. Mash cream cheese until soft and gradually beat in sugar and vanilla. Fold in whipped topping. Spread over crust. Spread blueberries on top. Chill overnight.

***

This luscious dessert turned out to be our son Alan's favorite, and he requested it every year for his birthday. Ron, however, graded it second to the bartender Vicki's apple squares.

Vicki's Harvest-Time Apple Squares

2 cups of flour
1 cup of packed brown sugar
¾ cup of granulated sugar
1 ½ teaspoons of cinnamon
½ cup of butter
1 cup of chopped walnuts
1 8 oz. pack of cream cheese, softened
2 tablespoons of milk
1 egg, beaten
½ teaspoon of vanilla
3 ½ cups of chopped apples

Combine flour, brown sugar, half a cup of granulated sugar and cinnamon. Cut in butter until a coarse texture forms. Stir in walnuts. Reserve two cups of the mix. Press remaining mix into nine-by-thirteen-inch pan. Combine cream cheese and milk. Mix until smooth. Add remaining quarter cup of sugar, egg, and vanilla. Mix well. Pour over crust. Top with remaining crumb mix. Bake at 350 degrees for thirty minutes. Chill before serving.

***

I met so many diverse people and made many dear friends while working in the bar, one in particular whom I fell in love with the minute I met him. Sam was in his eighties, a wiry, elfin little fellow who had only half of a nose and a perpetual twinkle in his eye. He was a retired surveyor and had kept a journal for over fifty years. He could tell you the temperature and humidity for any day from 1927 to 1982. He would come into the bar at precisely 11:00 a.m.

every day. He would order a beer, and I would drain all the prior day's empty liquor bottles into a shot glass for his daily cocktail. Can you imagine? Kahlúa, peppermint schnapps, gin, rum—whatever happened to be left in the bottom of the bottles.

At exactly noon, I would fetch Sam a bowl of Ada's soup of the day from the kitchen. This was most likely his only meal of the day. I would turn on the TV so he could watch the noon news. He didn't have a TV at home, and he enjoyed seeing the live news. In the summer, when he would show up with a five-pound bag of sugar, I knew that his raspberries were ready for me to pick so I could make his jam. I could set my clock by his arrival daily, and the day that he didn't show up, I sent one of the local firemen to his house to check on him. Jack found him peacefully at rest in his chair. He was sitting in front of the radio, listening to the baseball game. The dish of cookies that I had sent home with him was on the table next to his chair. Jack told me that he had a peaceful smile on his lips. "Wonders never cease" was his favorite expression. He gave me the best advice of my life at a time when I was in much need of guidance. I have passed his words of wisdom on to others on occasion: "When you don't know what to do, do nothing." I reminisce often about Sam and his common sense, prudence, and wit.

Sam was not the only one who loved Ada's soup. People came from miles to have her clam chowder on Fridays. Since I don't eat seafood, my favorite was her beef-barley soup on Wednesdays. When I tried to replicate her recipes and cut them down to a family-serving size, they just never turned out as good as hers. I would go to work early a couple of times a week just to watch her concoct her epicurean creations. When I questioned the fact that she never used a recipe, she just smiled and quoted a Canadian culinary author, Madame Benoît—"A recipe is only a theme that an intelligent cook can play each time with a variation." I think of this every time I make soup, and I laugh remembering when a customer asked me, "What is the soup of the day?" and I replied, "Barf-beely."

It is a wonder that I worked for this amazing lady for over eleven years, considering all the mishaps I encountered. One Friday, business in the bar was slow, so I went out to the restaurant to see if I could help out during the lunch rush. Someone ordered a cup of hot chocolate. The hot chocolate dispenser was directly over the soup vats. A waitress had just scooped out a bowl of clam chowder and hadn't put the cover back over the pot. Just as I pulled the lever to release the cocoa powder, the whole bottom of the machine gave way, and I gaped in horror as about two pounds of chocolate found its way into the clam chowder. I was frozen in shock, not knowing whether to laugh or cry.

When someone screamed, "Oh no!" I looked up and saw Ada coming out of the kitchen. She was, of course, furious.

The butter and cream and clams turned a pale brown as I slowly stirred the pot. "Could we possibly offer a special on chocolate chowder?" I lamely half-whispered.

Luckily, she had another pot of chowder to serve. If this wasn't grounds for dismissal, what would be?

Well, about six months later, I went into the walk-in cooler to get some beer. Instead of carrying out the whole case, I gingerly juggled three six-packs, one under my arm and one in each hand. As I reached for the door latch, I stumbled. One whole six-pack flew through air, landing with a crash on the rim of a huge pot of chili that was cooling nearby. I put down the other two six-packs and ran to the pot, only to see the foam from the beer and the broken glass slipping slowly to the bottom of Ada's prize-winning chili.

"Oh my god!" I wailed loud enough to be heard in the kitchen. I don't know what I expected him to do.

Sadly, there was not another pot of chili, so they ended up serving a commercial canned chili that day. I not only feared for my job but also was upset to think that Ada would never speak to me again. Her only words to me were "Will you please stay in the bar?" Of course, years later, we laughed about my clumsy mishaps.

I now use Ada's basic clam chowder recipe to make my cream of potato soup with a variation: bacon and no clams. You can, of course, add clams, fresh or canned, for a hearty clam chowder.

Cream of Potato Soup

Boil together in two quarts of salted water:

6 to 8 potatoes, diced   1 large white onion, chopped

Fry crisp and drain six slices of bacon, saving the bacon grease in pan. Add a quarter pound of butter to grease. Stir in three tablespoons of flour to make a rue.

Gradually stir in one cup of milk and one cup of heavy cream or evaporated milk. Drain half of the water from the potatoes and stir rue into potatoes and remaining water. Season with two chicken bouillon cubes and pepper to taste. Crumble bacon and add. For a delicious corn chowder, add frozen corn and simmer for about twenty minutes. To make soup thicker, if desired, take out a cupful of the liquid from the potatoes and thicken with more flour and stir back into hot soup.

***

Here is my version of Ada's mouthwatering beef-barley soup.

Beef-Barley Soup

1–2 pounds of diced lean beef   1 medium onion
4 cloves of garlic, crushed

Brown beef, onion, and garlic in vegetable oil. Add two quarts of water and let simmer for two to three hours.

Add the following:

3 carrots, sliced diagonally   4 stalks of celery, chopped
1 medium onion, chopped   2–3 sprigs of parsley
1 bay leaf   4 beef bouillon cubes
¾ cup of quick barley

Simmer for one hour or until vegetables are cooked. The last fifteen minutes, add a can of green beans and pepper to taste.

***

Ada also made a Waldorf salad for special occasions, and it has been my favorite to make when I want something unique to take to a party or an out-of-the-ordinary event. It is a little time-consuming but so worth it.

Waldorf Ring

⅓ cup of sugar   4 envelopes of unflavored gelatin
5 cups of white grape juice   3 medium stalks of celery
1 pound of seedless red grapes   3 medium Granny Smith apples (1 pound)
¾ cup of mayonnaise   ¼ cup of milk (I use evaporated milk)
1 cup walnuts, coarsely chopped

About four and a half hours before serving or a day ahead, in a four-quart saucepan, stir sugar and gelatin. Stir in two cups of white grape juice. Cook over medium heat, stirring frequently until gelatin is completely dissolved. Remove from heat. Stir in remaining grape juice. Refrigerate until mixture mounds when dropped from spoon (about forty-five minutes).

Meanwhile, chop celery. Cut each grape in half. When gelatin mixture almost comes to mounding consistency, quickly shred apples (apples will turn brown if shredded too early). Fold celery, grapes, and apples into gelatin mixture. Pour into a ten-inch Bundt pan or a ten-cup mold. Cover and refrigerate until set, at least three hours. Unmold on chilled platter.

Dressing: Mix mayonnaise and milk. Stir in walnuts. Serve with salad.

I love this salad, as does everyone who has tried it.

***

Linda was hired to tend bar shortly after I went to work at the Sportsman's Inn. She was tall, slender, and notably stylish. She was also raised in Montana. We became the best of friends over the years that we worked together, a friendship that has endured through many good times as well as bad for over forty years. Our kids attended school together, and we lived just blocks apart. We laugh today at the fact that we ever survived some of our shenanigans. We had a group of twelve, "the dirty dozen." Two of them were Linda's sisters.

On the last Friday of every month, which just happened to be our day off, we would all meet for lunch to celebrate whoever's birthday was that month. Linda and I usually started our day with breakfast and a coffee nudge (coffee, brandy, and Kahlúa) at the Sportsman's Inn and then go shopping until time to meet the gang for lunch. It was back to shopping after lunch. Some days we would shop until the mall closed and then stop at a Chinese restaurant on the way home. This particular establishment had a piano bar, and on several occasions, we were known to sing our hearts out and stay until closing. So by 2:30 a.m. and being several miles from home, it was only right that we would stop at Denny's for coffee and sometimes even breakfast. We'd usually get home about 4:00 a.m., sober, broke, and making plans for the next month.

Linda had an old boyfriend, Gordy, who owned a restaurant in one of the suburbs of Seattle. His signature salad was one that people raved about. He refused to divulge the dressing recipe to anyone. His restaurant, the Country Gentleman, burned to the ground sometime in the early 1990s.

"Just how did you get Gordy's recipe?" Linda questioned me. "I don't even have it!" she exclaimed.

I have been ever thankful for catching Gordy in a weak moment, probably after having had a little too much brandy.

***

Country Gentleman's Kona Salad

Dressing: ¾ cup of salad oil
¼ cup of sugar
1 teaspoon of Worcestershire sauce
2 tablespoons of grated onion
Salt and pepper (to taste)
¼ cup of white vinegar
⅓ cup of ketchup

Combine above ingredients and blend. Chill several hours.

Salad: 2 bunches of spinach

               8 slices of bacon, cooked crisp, crumbled

               3 hard-boiled eggs, chopped

               2 cups of fresh bean sprouts

               8 oz. can of sliced water chestnuts

               ½ small red onion, thinly sliced

Best spinach salad you will ever eat. *Delish!*

***

There was a fellow who stopped in the bar every summer. He had fruit orchards in Eastern Washington. Unbelievable as it seems, his name was Edsel Ford. Every year he would bring me bushels of fruit. I canned pears, peaches, apricots, cherries, and plums so all my friends and customers reaped the rewards of Edsel's generosity. Oh, how could I forget apples? We had oodles of apple pie and apple crisp.

Linda and I loved cooking together. We did catering for local weddings and parties and baked cakes for everyone's birthday or anniversary. Any special occasion was an excuse for us to bake. One of my favorite recipes of Linda's is her mom's pear marlow. It is a luscious marmalade, so easy to make, and great for gift-giving.

***

Pear Marlow

24 ripe pears, peeled

1 orange, ground in food processor

1 small can (8 ¼ oz.) of crushed pineapple

1 10 oz. bottle of Maraschino cherries, chopped

Add three quarter cups of sugar for each cup of the fruit mixture. Mix together and let stand all night. In the morning, boil mixture until it is clear. Put into hot sterilized jars and seal.

***

My neighbor Betty and I met through our landlord, Jack, who eventually became her husband. She was younger than me and had two adorable daughters. We talked recipes and kids day in and day out, laughed together until we cried, and became the closest of friends. She introduced me to what she called "real" cheesecake. She was from New Jersey, close enough to New York to know what the real thing was all about, baked and with eggs, not just cream cheese. It did turn out to be the best cheesecake I have ever eaten. Betty added many more recipes to my seemingly never-ending collection.

***

Real New York Cheesecake

3 8 oz. packages of cream cheese   1 cup of sugar
4 eggs   2 teaspoons of vanilla

Blend cream cheese and sugar thoroughly until smooth. Add one egg at a time, beating well after each one. Bake in a nine-by-nine-inch glass pan at 350 degrees for thirty minutes. Top may crack when taken out of oven. Top with canned cherry pie filling or make a glaze with fresh berries.

***

All of Betty's desserts were delectable. Her pies were juicy and succulent, and she made the best chocolate chip cookies ever (just ask Jack). Following are two of my favorite summer delicacies from her library of good things to eat. Both are quick and easy.

Peach Cobbler

Let stand for twenty minutes the following:

2 cups of sliced fresh peaches	¾ cup of sugar
1 cup of flour	1 cup of sugar
1 teaspoon of baking powder	1 cup of milk

Mix flour, sugar, baking powder, and milk and pour over peaches in a nine-inch square baking pan. Bake in 350-degree oven for thirty minutes or until bubbly and brown.

Rhubarb Crunch

Crumb topping:

1 cup of flour	¾ cup of uncooked oatmeal
1 cup of brown sugar	½ cup of melted butter
1 teaspoon of cinnamon	

Fruit mixture:

4 cups of diced rhubarb	1 cup of sugar
2 tablespoons of cornstarch	1 cup of water
1 teaspoon of vanilla	1 tablespoon of grated orange rind

Mix together crumb topping until crumbly. Press half into a nine-inch greased pan. Cover with rhubarb. In saucepan, combine sugar, cornstarch, water, and vanilla. Cook, stirring until clear and thick. Add orange rind. Pour over rhubarb. Cover with remaining crumb mix. Bake at 350 degrees for forty-five minutes. Serve warm with vanilla ice cream.

***

Try as I may, my chocolate chip cookies never held a candle to Betty's. That is, until I found this recipe, which supposedly came from a department store restaurant in Texas. After enjoying their lunch, the mother and daughter ordered a chocolate chip cookie for dessert. When they asked the waitress for the recipe, she replied that they didn't give it out, but they could purchase it for two fifty. They left smiling after signing the credit-card slip. When she received her bill, the charge from the restaurant was $285. She thought that she had paid $2.50 for the recipe. They refused to give her a refund, so she told them that she would get even by sending the recipe to anybody she could think of. She sent it to my friend Evelyn's sister, who sent it to her, and she, of course, shared it with me, so here it is.

$250 Chocolate Chip Cookies

1 cup of butter
1 teaspoon of baking powder
1 teaspoon of baking soda
2 ½ cups of oatmeal, processed until powdery
2 cups of flour
1 cup of granulated sugar
1 cup of brown sugar
½ teaspoon of salt
2 eggs
1 teaspoon of vanilla
12 ounces of chocolate chips
½ 8 oz. Hershey baking bar (grated)
1 ½ cups of chopped nuts

Cream together butter and both sugars. Add eggs and vanilla. Mix together with flour, oatmeal, salt, baking powder, and soda. Add chocolate chips, grated Hershey bar, and nuts. Roll into balls and place two inches apart on a cookie sheet. Bake for ten minutes at 375 degrees.

***

Betty also made a killer pound cake. She told me that it was Elvis Presley's favorite cake. I have no reason to doubt that. This cake freezes well, which makes it convenient when you have unexpected guests pop in for coffee.

Elvis Presley Pound Cake

7 eggs
3 cups of flour
3 cups of sugar
2 teaspoons of vanilla
½ pound of butter (no margarine allowed)
1 cup of whipping cream (to be added last)

Cream eggs, sugar, and butter and then add the flour and vanilla. Last, fold in whipping cream.

Do not preheat oven. Pour into greased Bundt pan and place in cold oven. Turn heat on to 350 degrees. Bake for one hour. *Do not open oven during baking time.* If cake does not appear done, bake for another ten minutes or until done.

***

The first spring after I met Betty, she appeared at my door on Saint Patrick's Day with a large platter of something that looked like midget potatoes. There is an old Irish proverb that says, "You must take the little potato with the big potato." I never understood the meaning of it, as with many Irish proverbs, but that is all I could think of as I gazed at her offering.

I began to laugh as she explained to me, "These are Irish potatoes, and I make them every Saint Patrick's Day."

What looked to be dirt turned out to be cinnamon, and after just one bite, I couldn't stop eating them. The recipe was passed down from

Otto Glaser, who was the president of Dairy Maid Confectionery Company in Philadelphia in the 1950s. Betty surprised me with these again just a few years ago.

Cinnamon Irish Potatoes

Pour one and a half pints of water into a kettle. Add three pounds of granulated sugar and eight ounces of white corn syrup. Stir over flame until sugar is dissolved and mixture starts to boil and then stop stirring. Wait ten minutes and then drop a small amount into cold water. When it forms a soft ball (softball stage is 235 to 240 degrees), take mixture off heat. Set kettle in cold water to cool and then beat until creamy. Remove from kettle and fold in one and a half pounds of shredded coconut and one teaspoon of vanilla extract. Roll mixture on table, cut into small pieces, shape into balls, and roll in cinnamon. Place on wax paper and let set two hours. Makes five pounds.

This takes a lot of beating to get the creamy consistency and a lot of self-control to let set for two hours. Every bite is delicious.

Chapter 7

A lesson well learned from my years of bartending was to never judge people. I also quickly caught on that a prudent bartender knows absolutely nothing about her customers. "Oh, do you have a brother?" would be my comeback if someone asked me who their brother left with the night before. I always wore a wedding ring as every guy's second question after "What's your name?" was "Are you married?"

"What difference does it make? You are" was always my glib response. Most of the time, I was right.

Life was finally falling into a placid place for me. The kids were settled into their new school, I had a good-paying job (even if not what I had planned on for a career) and we had a warm, comfortable, affordable home. I was getting just enough child support to cover my rent, so my utilities, car, and food budget all had to be covered by my wages. Thank god for tips! My tips paid for gas and school lunches, and any spending money I could squeeze out for the two teenagers, I was trying to provide for. Looking back on those times now, I am amused, wondering how I ever managed.

A new dome stadium, the Kingdome, was built in Seattle in 1976, and the opening day for the newly franchised Seattle Mariners was set for April 6, 1977, Easter Sunday. I was elated when one of my customers offered to take me and the kids to the ball game. My daughter was not so thrilled.

"Why would we spend Easter Sunday at a dumb baseball game?" she wailed.

She pouted all the way to Seattle. It turned out that she enjoyed the game more than any of us and was, from that day forward, an avid Mariners fan. I managed to juggle my finances to allow for at least one baseball game a week. General admission at that time was only

$3, and I would pile my kids and as many neighbor kids as we could fit into the car, and away we would go.

By the time Christmas rolled around that year, I knew that I wasn't going to be able to afford much for the kids. My dad, ever my hero, came to the rescue when he called on Thanksgiving to ask if we would like to spend Christmas in Montana with him and my mom. I had not been home for the holidays since I left Butte twenty years earlier. He was buying us train tickets for our Christmas gift. The kids were beaming with excitement; they had never been on a train.

On the day we were scheduled to leave, there was a freight-train derailment on Stevens Pass. We ended up having to take a bus to Spokane, where we spent the night in the historical Davenport Hotel to await the train going east the next day. Having dinner in the extravagant hotel dining room, which was breathtakingly decorated, was only a start to one of my most memorable Christmases. We awoke in the morning to a picturesque winter wonderland.

The news that we would be delayed until late that night was not what the passengers wanted to hear. Everyone was anxious to get to their destination for Christmas. We bundled up and walked to the center of town, where the snow was falling, folks were hustling, Christmas lights were glowing, and carols were floating through the air. It was all like a dream or a movie, and it is a memory that replays itself in my mind every Christmas. It turned out that we had to take a bus the rest of the way to Butte. When we arrived at the bus station on Christmas Eve, my eyes widened in surprise, and I squealed in disbelief when I saw my eldest son, Patrick, waiting there to meet us. He had driven an old beat-up Volkswagen Bug all the way from Missouri to spend Christmas with us. I couldn't have asked for a more perfect holiday. The kids weren't too disappointed about not getting to ride the train. We did get to take it back to Washington.

On Easter Sunday—March 26, 1978—my beautiful granddaughter Nicole was born. How could I be a grandmother at thirty-eight years of age? It was a rainy, gloomy morning when the phone call woke me. I hurried the kids into my rickety old car with bald tires and whispered a prayer that we could make it the seventy-some miles to Puyallup. Somewhere along the way, in the pouring rain, we picked up a hitchhiker and his large wet stinky dog.

The proud new dad, Patrick, greeted us at the hospital entrance with a smile that will live in my heart forever. My son Don was there also and had somehow talked the nurse into letting him hold the baby up to the nursery window to show her off to the family. He was beaming as much as his brother. A feeling of breathlessness overcame me as I gazed at this beautiful little miracle. This was just the beginning of my new life as a grandma. Many, many years and many more children have yet to dim the thrill of how I feel when I hold one of my new loves.

Barely two months after Nicole was born, I lost my dad. He was not only my hero but also my biggest fan. It didn't matter what I did growing up; it was always the best in my pa's eyes. I was the best singer in the choir. I was the best dancer, the best student. I grew up confident of everything I ever did because of his never-ending encouragement and approval. It was hard to even imagine life without him. I didn't cry when he passed, but three months later, on Father's Day, I had a meltdown. I buried my face in my hands and sobbed for what seemed like hours. Not a day goes by, even after all these years, that I don't wish I could have just one more day with him.

One evening, shortly after my dad passed away, my boss called to inform me that the night-shift bartender had not shown up, so I would have to fill in. I had never worked a night shift, and it was a Friday night, bound to be busy.

I could hear my dad's voice teasing me, "You're not a slow bartender, and you're not a fast bartender. You are a 'half-fast' bartender." Well, this was to be my test.

Things were going well, and I seemed to be doing a pretty good job keeping up with the crowd. There was only one vacant barstool, way at the end of the bar. In walked a lone stranger.

I hurriedly set out a coaster, hardly even glancing at this dude, and asked, "What would you like?"

"You" came the aggravating retort.

"What can I get you to drink?" I snapped back.

"Double orange juice on the rocks."

His voice and the words he had just spoken took me so by surprise that I was forced to actually look at him. I tried all night to ignore him, but he kept calling me back, questioning me and then questioning the customers about me. Although he was getting on my nerves, I kept reminding myself, *At least he's not drinking.*

As soon as the rush calmed down and he got my attention, he gave me a long narration about what a great guy he was. He was amusing with a sharp, sarcastic sense of humor, even if a bit egotistical.

"Well, what do you think about me?" he gingerly questioned me.

"I think you are the most arrogant bastard I've ever met" was my rude response as I walked away, avoiding eye contact.

The following weekend when he showed up at the end of my Friday day shift, I mustered up a smile and apologized for my disrespectful comeback the week before. He laughed, telling me that he was actually impressed with my spunky reaction to his first attempt to bedazzle me.

Larry and I became good friends over the next two years. His children and mine were in the same age group, and they enjoyed spending weekends together. We would take the kids out for pizza on Friday nights or have a weenie roast and make s'mores at his campsite. If I knew they would be stopping by the house on a Saturday morning, I would be sure and have my aromatic banana bread baking in the oven. I think he fell in love with my cooking.

***

The Best Banana Bread

2 cups of flour

½ teaspoon of salt

1 cup of sugar

1 teaspoon of vanilla

1 cup of chopped nuts

2 teaspoons of baking soda

½ cup of butter

2 eggs

3 large or 4 small bananas

Measure and sift flour, soda, salt. Cream butter and sugar; add eggs and vanilla. Stir until thoroughly mixed. Stir in mashed bananas. Fold in dry ingredients and nuts. Pour in well-greased loaf pan. Bake at 350 degrees for fifty-five minutes to an hour.

***

Larry finally mustered up enough courage to ask me if I would like to go to a movie with him. *Annie Hall* was playing, and I wanted to see it but wasn't sure that I was ready for a date. When he added "dinner," I knew it was officially a date.

"Well," I hesitantly replied, "okay, pick me up at six o'clock."

My friend Edsel had just dropped off a bushel of apples, so I decided that I would have a freshly baked apple pie made when Larry arrived. I had an hour to get ready after putting the pie in the oven. I walked across the street to my neighbor Betty's to borrow something spiffy to wear as I only had work clothes. The pie overflowed in the oven, causing the smoke alarm to go off in my house. Hearing the alarm, I quickly ran back. As I was trying to clean up the mess in the oven, my "date" showed up at the door, exactly one hour early. I was in my jeans, hair uncombed, on my knees in front of the smoking oven and an uncooked pie.

"Aren't you ready yet?" He smirked.

The basket of apples was just within my reach, and without hesitation, I heaved one and then another in his direction. He was laughing and dodging them, and I was fuming.

"Being early is so rude," I admonished him as I was mentally ordering myself to calm down.

After all was said and done, it turned out to be a great evening. He somehow always made me smile.

Larry loved to dance, and there was a band that played on weekends at the tavern across from where I worked. One Friday night, he cajoled me into going there when I got off work. I too loved to dance and hadn't been dancing in many years. He had a girlfriend, Carol, who worked nights, milking cows at a nearby dairy. Her shift was over at midnight, so I knew that when the band started playing "The Midnight Hour," it was time for me to leave. I was all right with that.

After a few weeks of really enjoying swing dancing, the band played and sang Anne Murray's "You Needed Me." As I listened to the words and felt Larry's arms around me, I all of a sudden hated Carol.

And besides, she always smells like cow poop! my brain screamed.

I left that night with a painful tightness in my throat, feeling sad and lonely.

In the spring of 1979, on my thirty-ninth birthday, I mustered up the nerve to tell Larry that he deserved much better than Carol. He kind of smirked, informing me that I had been blind to the fact that she had been a thing of the past for some time. In August, we eloped to Reno on his motorcycle, which, up until then, I wouldn't even get on.

Our families were shocked. I hadn't met his parents, nor had my mother met him. My mother's first words when I called her were "A good Irish Catholic girl marring a Dutch Jew? Good luck." Her message to him was, "Don't ever tell her that she can't do something, and don't talk to her in the morning before she has had her coffee." Good advice, Mom.

We now had a family with five teenagers. I can't say in all honesty that it was an easy transition for the kids, but we all made it through, and I feel so fortunate for having added to my family at that time. Our kids were compatible and close in age, and I felt such a sense of pride introducing his children—Jay, Alan, and Julie—as mine. It did turn out to be "the more the merrier" over the years.

Being a bachelor for ten years, Larry had his own ideas of cooking and food in general. The first thing that he requested for breakfast was foreign to me—"graveyard stew." He explained that it was what the longshoremen in Seattle ate at the local skid-row greasy spoon for breakfast after working their night shift. It is still—and I suppose will always be—his favorite comfort food.

***

Graveyard Stew

3 poached eggs
½ cup of milk, scalded
Salt and pepper to taste

3 slices of dark toasted bread
2 tablespoons of butter

Break toast into scalded milk, top with poached eggs, butter, and season. That's it!

***

Larry talked a lot about his grandmother's cooking. When he mentioned that she made a chocolate cake with mayonnaise, I thought he was pulling my leg, but he found her recipe, and I reluctantly made it. I have to admit it is good if you like chocolate.

Mayonnaise Cake

1 cup of raisins or chopped dates
1 cup of hot water

1 cup of walnuts
1 teaspoon of baking soda

Add baking soda to hot water and pour over raisins or dates and walnuts. Let stand for a few minutes. In the meantime, combine the following:

1 cup of sugar
½ cup of cocoa
1 teaspoon of cinnamon
¾ cup of mayonnaise

½ teaspoon of salt
2 cups of flour
1 teaspoon of vanilla

Mix ingredients thoroughly. Bake in nine-by-thirteen-inch greased pan at 350-degree oven for forty-five minutes.

***

A 1935 note from Grandma Belle reads, "This tasty cake serves eight to eighteen generously. Keeps extremely well and may be frosted or not as you choose."

When Larry asked me for "a poor man's steak sandwich," I looked at him blankly. I had no inkling as to what he was talking about. He explained to me that it is, in fact, no more than a fried egg sandwich on white bread. His other favorite lunchtime treat was peanut butter and dill pickle sandwiches. As much as I love peanut butter, I couldn't imagine it with dill pickles.

Sometime in the early 1980s, I joined a popular weight-loss program. I did well with the food planning but was continuously talking about food—when to eat, what to eat, how much to eat. The plan involved a lot of weighing and measuring of the food you consumed. This became second nature to me. My favorite part of the weekly meeting was the recipe exchange. I had a large bulging binder full of "skinny" recipes, as we called them. I was anxious to try a new dish every week, and my husband was always willing to try something different. Most of the time, he ate whatever I cooked and never complained. If he didn't like something, he might suggest that I not make it again. It was an altogether different story, however, the day I served him my prune-noodle casserole.

He took one bite, looked up at me with something near horror in his eyes, and blurted out in a defensive tone of voice, "I don't have to eat this shit!"

I laughed so hard that I spit my mouthful of prunes and noodles across the table.

From that day forward, he was always leery when he saw me looking through that binder. Nope, I didn't save the recipe, nor did I ever share it with anyone.

***

There was a contest in our area for a recipe using a particular brand of yogurt. I concocted my yummy yogurt waffles, going so far as to breaking down the food points. It was a hit with my group as well as my family and won me six months' worth of coupons for yogurt. This is also our traditional family Christmas morning fare.

Yummy Yogurt Fruit Waffles

2 eggs	1 cup of all-purpose flour
¼ teaspoon of salt	½ teaspoon of baking soda
½ teaspoon of baking powder	1 8 oz. container of plain yogurt
1 medium banana	⅓ cup of vegetable oil

Beat eggs until light. Sift together flour, salt, baking soda, and baking powder. Blend yogurt and banana together until smooth. Add flour mixture alternately with yogurt-banana mixture. Fold in beaten eggs. Add vegetable oil. Mix only until blended. Bake in preheated waffle iron.

Topping: Combine six ounces of nondairy whipped topping with one eight-ounce container of strawberry yogurt. Add one quart of sliced fresh or frozen strawberries and one sliced banana. Spoon topping over warm waffles. Serves four.

The version we have on Christmas morning is made with a quart of strawberry ice cream in place of the whipped nondairy topping. Yummy!

***

The recipes I used most often during my weight-regime period were salad creations that I have continued to use throughout the years and have shared with many. Here are just a few of my favorites.

Shape-Up Fitness Salad

This salad is best made in a glass bowl, which shows each layer and makes it quite appealing. It can be made with or without the shrimp and is equally tasty either way. I, of course, make it without.

3–4 stalks of celery, sliced
3 slender carrots, thinly sliced
1 can of sliced water chestnuts
1 10 oz. package of frozen peas (do not thaw)
1 medium bunch of radishes, sliced
1 bunch of green onions, sliced
6 oz. package of frozen shrimp (or 2 small cans, drained)
1 head of lettuce, torn in bite-sized pieces (combine iceberg, romaine, green, and red for color)

Dressing:

1 ½ cups of mayonnaise or salad dressing
1–2 tablespoons of sugar (optional)
2–4 hard-cooked eggs
8 ounces of grated Swiss cheese
Mushrooms
Cherry tomatoes

Layer first eight ingredients in large glass bowl in order listed. Gently spread mayonnaise over top and sprinkle with sugar if desired. Cover and marinate at least four hours or overnight. Before serving, dig deep to mix slightly or turn into bowl and toss. Garnish with sieved hard-cooked eggs, grated Swiss cheese, sliced mushrooms, and cherry tomatoes.

Crunchy Vegetable Salad

1 pound of fresh broccoli 1 small head of cauliflower
3 carrots (thinly sliced) 3 stalks of celery (sliced)
1 green pepper (coarsely chopped) 1 red pepper or pimento (for color)

Dressing:

½ cup of sugar 1 teaspoon of dry mustard
1 teaspoon of salt ¼ cup of vinegar
½ cup of vegetable oil 1 small onion, grated
1 teaspoon of poppy seeds

Cover salad and allow to marinate in refrigerator overnight. Drain well before serving

Asian Chicken Salad

1 chicken breast, cooked and shredded
½ large head of cabbage, shredded
4 green onions, chopped
2 tablespoons of sesame seeds
½ cup of slivered almonds
2 packages of Top Ramen noodles (chicken flavored)

Dressing:

3 tablespoons of vinegar 1 teaspoon of salt
½ teaspoon of pepper 3 tablespoons of sugar
½ cup of oil Chicken-flavored packet from noodles
½ teaspoon of Accent (optional)

Mix cabbage, chicken, and onion with dressing and allow to marinate several hours or overnight. Place sesame seeds and almond on a shallow pan and brown in a 350-degree oven for five to ten minutes.

Let cool and add to noodles. Add to cabbage mixture and toss just before serving.

Oriental Shrimp Salad

1 10 oz. package of frozen peas
1 ½ pounds of cooked, peeled shrimp
¼ cup of chopped onion
1 tablespoon of soy sauce
1 teaspoon of sugar
2 teaspoons of curry powder
½ teaspoon of celery seeds
12 cherry tomatoes

½ cup plus 2 teaspoons of instant rice
1 ½ cups of diced celery
½ pound of fresh mushrooms, sliced
½ cup of salad oil
3 tablespoons of cider vinegar
¼ cup of slivered almonds
Small can of artichoke hearts

Cook peas and rice in separate pans according to package directions. Drain. In large glass or enamel bowl, mix peas, rice, shrimp, celery, onion, and mushrooms. In another bowl, combine soy sauce, sugar, curry powder, almonds, celery seeds, salad oil, and vinegar. Pour over the other ingredients. Chill several hours. Serve surrounded by artichoke hearts and cherry tomatoes.

***

The first Thanksgiving in our new home, I decided to have a special brunch and invite my friend Linda and her husband, Jack. I fastidiously planned the ideal menu, brought out the fancy china, which I hadn't used in years, and ordered a fresh flower centerpiece. I wanted it all to be picture-perfect as it was our first time entertaining. It turned out as lovely as I had hoped it would and became our annual holiday celebration with our friends for many years. Linda and I took turns hosting, but the menu always remained the same.

Pumpkin Puff Pancakes

2 eggs

½ cup of canned pumpkin

2 tablespoons of sugar

½ teaspoon of nutmeg

¼ cup of salad oil

1 cup pf milk

1 ¾ cups of pancake mix

½ teaspoon of cinnamon

½ teaspoon of ginger

Beat eggs until thick and lemon colored. Stir in remaining ingredients. Pour batter by tablespoon onto medium-hot ungreased griddle. Bake until puffed and bubbles begin to break. Turn and bake on other side until golden brown. Makes about five dozen two-inch pancakes.

Serve with warm rum-flavored maple syrup. Heat one cup of maple syrup and one tablespoon of butter. Remove from heat and stir in half a teaspoon of rum flavoring. Serve warm.

***

We still today have these scrumptious little cakes every Thanksgiving with sausage balls (the size of a marble shooter) and scrambled eggs. As a side dish, I serve a fresh fruit cup or an ambrosia of orange, grapefruit, and pineapple sprinkled with coconut.

With the remainder of the canned pumpkin, I usually whip up some pumpkin spice muffins, which freeze well and are delicious served warm for breakfast.

Pumpkin Spice Muffins

1 cup of canned pumpkin

1 cup of sugar

1 cup of vegetable oil

½ cup of buttermilk

2 eggs

1 ⅔ cups of flour

1 teaspoon of cinnamon

½ teaspoon of cloves

¼ teaspoon of ginger

¼ teaspoon of allspice

1 teaspoon of baking soda

½ teaspoon of salt

1 cup of chopped nuts (if desired)

Combine pumpkin, sugar, oil, buttermilk, and eggs. Beat for one minute. Add dry ingredients. Mix thoroughly until mixture is moistened. Don't over-stir. Fold in nuts. Line twelve muffin cups with paper liners. Pour batter into cups, filling two-thirds full. Bake for twenty to twenty-five minutes in preheated four-hundred-degree oven. Serve while warm.

Chapter 8

We awoke to what sounded like a sonic boom. The dining room windows clattered as if to explode at any moment. Mount Saint Helens had erupted. It was May 18, 1980. Although the mountain was almost six hundred miles from our front door, we experienced not only the initial shock but also curtains of ash that covered our trees and created an eerie sense of darkness. It was reported to be the deadliest and most destructive volcano eruption in the history of the United States. Fifty-seven people perished that morning, including one Harry Randall Truman, the eighty-three-year-old owner and caretaker of the Spirit Lake lodge, who stubbornly refused to leave his home when told to evacuate days before.

This was just one of the many memorable events of the 1980 era. There were assassination attempts on President Reagan and Pope John Paul. Sally Ride was the first American woman to conquer space. Michael Jackson topped the pop charts with "Thriller," and we all joined hands to chant "We Are the World." Every little girl was hoping for a Cabbage Patch Kid for Christmas, and the boys and some grown men were overcome with Pac-Man fever. We swooned over Patrick Swayze in *Dirty Dancing* and held our breath as we ventured *Back to the Future*. Oh, the marvelous, wondrous eighties.

This was a turning time in our lives as our children were all grown and making their own way in the world. From 1984 to 1989, we were blessed with five granddaughters and two grandsons. Our family gatherings were growing every year. Our annual Easter egg hunt became one of our favorite events. We would fill plastic eggs with prize numbers and coins and candy and hide them over our parklike landscaped one-acre yard. One year, my son Don put a baby frog in one of the eggs and showed Nicole, our eldest granddaughter, where it was. When she opened it and that frog jumped out, she leaped in the air, higher than the frog, and screamed hysterically as we all watched and laughed.

Another memorable year, I bought a huge Easter egg piñata. No one told me that you had to fill it. I thought that they came preloaded. We hung it high in a tree and let the kids take turns, smallest first, hitting it with a broomstick. After several swats, when it finally burst open and nothing came out, the kids all looked around, eyes widening in confusion. Frowning and perplexed, they turned to me in disbelief. What could I say?

"Oops."

The children all balked as the adults turned away, bursting out in uncontrollable laughter.

Sometime in the mid-eighties, my husband bought our first IBM home computer. I was uncertain of this new technology and swore that it could never replace my trusty old Remington typewriter. It took me about eighteen months to work up the courage to even try to figure it out.

At about the same time, I became involved in a home-party-plan company. I agreed to book and hold parties to sell Christmas merchandise. I thought it would be a great way to make a little extra money and earn gifts for my own holiday giving. Little did I know when I signed on the bottom line that this part-time job would take me to corners of the world that, up until that time, I had only dreamed of visiting. I was still working full-time, but I immersed myself into this new venture, determined to earn the breathtaking trips that the company offered. The goals that I set seemed unreachable. The hours of work and determination paid off well as over a nine-year period with the company, I was able to travel to Hawaii, Greece, Italy, Brazil, and Egypt and enjoy Mexican and Caribbean cruises. My trips were all expenses paid, and I had only to pay $1,000 each trip to take my husband along. These were first-class dream excursions that we would never have been able to afford. The company also paid for my training trips to Florida and Kansas City every year. I worked all this in with my regular job. Oh, life was good in the eighties.

Another bonus I derived from this job was the new people I met and all my old friends encouraging me and working with me. Even my sister, who lived in Nevada, joined my venture. She enjoyed the social side of the job, and it was good to see her involved in something to keep her busy. It was also a great chance for us to spend more time together.

The weekly training meetings that I held with my new associates turned into wonderful food-filled gatherings. Brunch at the Hewett home was akin to Christmas every day. We all looked forward to sharing our favorite dishes. The following brunch casserole is most favorable as it can be made ahead and baked just before serving.

Easy Brunch Casserole

1 12 oz. package of link sausage
6 English muffins, cut into one-inch cubes
¼ cup of butter, melted
½ cup of chopped red pepper
12 eggs
2 cups of milk
½ teaspoon of salt
½ teaspoon of pepper
½ cup of chopped onion
¼ cup of bacon bits
1 cup of shredded cheddar cheese
1 cup of shredded mozzarella cheese

Cook sausage according to package directions. Cool slightly; cut into quarter-inch slices. Place English muffin cubes in a greased thirteen-by-nine-inch baking dish; drizzle with butter. Layer with sausage, cheese, onion, and red pepper. In a large bowl, combine the eggs, milk, salt, and pepper. Pour over cheese. Sprinkle with bacon. Cover and refrigerate overnight. Remove from the refrigerator thirty minutes before baking. Uncover and bake at 350 degrees for forty-five to fifty minutes or until a knife inserted into center comes out clean. Let stand five minutes before serving. Serves twelve.

***

A great accompaniment dish for breakfast, lunch, or dinner and easy to prepare for a potluck or quick meal at home is made with frozen hash browns.

Cheesy Baked Hash Browns

2 pounds of shredded frozen hash browns (thawed)
½ cup of chopped onion
¼ cup of melted butter
2 cups of grated cheddar cheese
1 can of cream-of-chicken soup
1 cup of sour cream
Crushed potato chips
Salt and pepper to taste

Mix hash browns, onion, butter, salt, and pepper. Place in nine-by-thirteen-inch greased baking pan. Mix soup and sour cream and pour over potatoes. Spread cheese over top and sprinkle generously with potato chips. Bake, uncovered, in 350-degree oven for one hour.

***

Be it brunch or an evening potluck, you could count on my "Christmas Around the World" girls to come through with some tasty dishes.

Chicken in the Weeds

1 32 oz. package of frozen broccoli (cooked)
2 cups of cooked, chopped chicken breast
2 cans of cream-of-chicken soup
1 cup of mayonnaise

2 tablespoons of lemon juice
½ teaspoon of Worcestershire sauce
1 teaspoon of curry powder
1 cup of grated cheddar cheese

Place broccoli in a two-quart greased casserole. Mix soup, mayonnaise, lemon juice, Worcestershire sauce, and curry powder. Pour half of mixture over broccoli. Layer chicken on top. Pour remaining mixture over and top with cheese. Sprinkle half a cup of breadcrumbs mixed with two tablespoons of butter over top and bake at 350 degrees for thirty to forty-five minutes.

***

Everyone's favorite finger food was a dish that my friend Mary made on several occasions. It didn't have a name, so whenever my dear friend David wanted me to make it for a get-together or a party at work years later, he would always ask if I would make "that white shit." My boss finally asked me one day if we couldn't please give it a name. David suggested *"caca blanca,"* which is Spanish for what he had been calling it all along. So to this day, that is its designated title. It is always a hit and probably my most shared recipe.

Caca Blanca

Spread two packages of crescent roll dough flat on cookie sheet and bake at 375 degrees for about ten minutes or until brown. Cool.

Mix the following:

2 8 oz. packages of cream cheese
1 cup of mayonnaise
1 package of Hidden Valley Ranch mix (original)

Spread on cooled crust and sprinkle with the following:

Chopped broccoli   Chopped cauliflower
Grated carrots   Grated cheddar cheese

**

Another popular take-along treat was Angie's poppy seed bread. We use to joke about not passing a drug test after eating a couple of slices of this flavorful quick bread. It is so easy to make; just mix all the ingredients and bake. It makes two generous loaves, one to take and one to keep.

Poppy Seed Bread

3 cups of flour   1 ½ teaspoons of salt
2 ¼ cups of sugar   1 ½ teaspoons of vanilla
1 ½ teaspoons of baking powder   3 eggs
1 ½ tablespoons of poppy seeds   1 ½ teaspoons of butter flavoring
1 ½ teaspoons of almond extract   1 ½ cups of milk
1 ½ cups of oil

Mix all ingredients together and pour into two greased and floured loaf pans. Bake at 350 degrees for about one hour. Remove from pan and let cool for about one hour.

Topping: ¾ cup of sugar   ¼ cup of orange juice
           ½ teaspoon of vanilla   ½ teaspoon of almond extract
           ½ teaspoon of butter flavoring

Boil ingredients and pour topping over cooled loaves.

**

In 1990, a new Pay 'n Save drugstore opened in Monroe. I decided that it was time to pursue a new career after tending bar for eleven years.

My mother laughed at me. "They don't hire fifty-year-olds."

Well, I did get the job and worked for the company for thirteen years. I discovered that I loved retail work, and my coworkers all became like family to me. The workplace was again the perfect setting for sharing recipes and discovering new and delicious food. My new coworkers just happened to be some of the best cooks I had ever met. Neva's "better than sex" cake turned out to be exactly what she promised. When I told her that I didn't eat chocolate, she even came up with a pineapple variety.

***

Better-Than-Sex Cake — Chocolate

4 eggs
1 cup of sour cream
½ cup of oil
1 cup of semisweet chocolate chips
¼ cup of water
¾ cup of chopped pecans
1 teaspoon of vanilla
1 package of chocolate butter cake mix
1 four-serving box of chocolate instant pudding

Mix all ingredients except chocolate chips and pecans for three minutes. Fold in chocolate chips and pecans. Bake in greased and floured tube or Bundt pan at 350 degrees for forty-five to fifty minutes. Cool for ten minutes. Remove from pan. Frost when cool.

Frosting

1 pound of powdered sugar   ¾ stick of butter
3 1 oz. squares of baking chocolate,   MilkCream butter and half of the
melted   powdered sugar until fluffy.

Blend in chocolate. Add remaining sugar and enough milk (one tablespoon at a time) to desired consistency. Frost cooled cake.

Better-Than-Sex Cake — Pineapple

    1 package of yellow cake mix
    2 cups of milk
    1 20 oz. can of crushed pineapple
    1 8 oz. frozen whipped topping, thawed
    ½ cup of sugar
    1 3 oz. can of flaked coconut
    1 four-serving box of vanilla instant pudding
    1 cup of chopped nuts

Make cake as directed on box using eggs, water, and oil called for. Bake in greased and floured nine-by-thirteen-inch pan at 350 degrees following time chart on box. Cool for twenty-five minutes.

Simmer pineapple and sugar for five minutes. Poke holes in cake with wooden skewer or toothpick. Pour pineapple mixture over cake and cool completely. Mix pudding mix and milk. Allow to thicken. Spread pudding on cake and refrigerate fifteen to twenty minutes. Spread with whipped topping and sprinkle with coconut and nuts. Refrigerate overnight.

***

Second best to this pineapple epicurean delight is the following Kahlúa cake, which I made especially for my friend Elsie on her birthday.

Kahlúa Cake

1 package of devil's food cake mix
1 cup of sour cream
¾ cup of vegetable oil
1 cup of chopped nuts
4 eggs
1 cup of Kahlúa liqueur
1 6 oz. package of chocolate chips

In large bowl, combine cake mix, eggs, sour cream, Kahlúa and oil. Blend at low speed and then beat three to five minutes at medium speed. Stir in chocolate chips and nuts. Pour into greased and floured ten-inch Bundt pan. Bake at 350 degrees for fifty-five to sixty minutes until toothpick inserted in center comes out clean. Cool on rack for thirty minutes. Remove from pan and cool completely. Dust with powdered sugar or serve with whipped cream.

***

As a carryover from my bartending days, I decided to treat my coworkers to my legendary rum cake. It was such a hit that it became my signature cake, and I ended up making it for every Christmas party.

Dark Rum Cake

1 cup of chopped pecans or walnuts
1 package of yellow cake mix
4 eggs
½ cup of cold water
½ cup of vegetable oil
½ cup of dark rum
1 four-serving package of instant vanilla pudding

Sprinkle nuts over bottom of greased ten-inch tube pan or twelve-cup Bundt pan. Pour batter over nuts. Bake at 325 degrees for twenty-five to thirty minutes. Let cool in pan for ten minutes. Remove from pan.

Glaze: ¼ pound of butter   ¼ cup of water
         1 cup of granulated sugar   ½ cup of dark rum

Melt butter, stir in water and sugar, and boil, stirring constantly for five minutes or until sugar is completely dissolved. Stir in rum. Pour over cake while still warm.

***

Every year, I insisted on getting a permit to cut down a live Christmas tree, and every year, it became more of a disaster than the year before.

"No, I don't like the shape of that one."

"Well, the one you want is too tall."

"Just pick one, cut the damned thing down, and get it over with."

Christmas cheer abounded. By the time we would get the tree home, we usually weren't even speaking, or I was in tears.

"Why do you go through this every year?" my boss questioned me. "Just send him to get it alone and be satisfied with whatever he chooses."

It was not easy for me to do, but I decided it might be more pleasant than our annual knock-down-drag-out. Larry could not believe that I wasn't going with him to get a tree. I told him to go while I was at work. I came home to what had to be the most hideous tree in the forest. One side was flat.

"Well, I guess that side can go against the wall." I sighed.

Whichever way I turned it, there was a bare spot.

I am not going to bitch or complain, I told myself as I bit my lip to hold back the tears.

He had put it in the tree stand right in the middle of the dining room floor. I had to walk around it to get to any room in the house. There it stood, waiting to be moved to a designated spot. I was not about to move it. I thought if I waited long enough, he would find a proper place for it. I finally watered it, and we gingerly walked around it until the day before Christmas Eve.

As I was leaving for work, I saw a shotgun shell sitting on the shelf. I put a red ribbon around it and tied it onto a limb on the ugly, undecorated, misplaced tree. I was sure this would encourage Larry to decorate it when he arrived home. He called me at work, not a bit amused, to ask me if that shotgun shell was a hint that I wanted to shoot him.

I sweetly replied, "No, dear," with a giggle in my voice. "It's just 'a cartridge in a bare tree.'"

We laughed together as we decorated the tree that evening, our most unforgettable Christmas tree ever.

***

In spite of all the Christmas cookies I had made over the years, I had never attended a cookie exchange. When the ladies at work planned one, I was so excited. I only had to bake ten dozen of one kind of cookie and would go home with a dozen of ten different kinds of cookies. What a genius idea. I don't even remember what kind of cookies I took, probably holly doodles, which are just snickerdoodles rolled in red and green sugar sprinkles instead of cinnamon sugar. I do remember, however, how delighted I was to see so many new cookie ideas. The best part of my holiday baking, to this day, is reading the recipes on the cards that we also exchanged. Do people even do cookie exchanges today? Here are a few of my favorites.

Shirley's No-Bake Cookies

2 cups of sugar
½ cup of cocoa
½ cup of milk
2 ½ cups of oatmeal

½ cup of peanut butter (chunky or smooth)
½ cup of butter
½ teaspoon of vanilla

Combine sugar, cocoa, butter, and milk. Boil for one to two minutes. Remove from heat. Stir in peanut butter, oats, and vanilla. Drop by rounded teaspoons onto wax paper.

Sally's Grandma's Chocolate Treats

1 6 oz. package of semisweet chocolate chips
1 6 oz. package of butterscotch chips
1 can (regular size) of Chinese noodles
6 ounces of cashew halves or quarters

Melt the chips together in a double boiler and stir until blended. Remove pan from water bath and add nuts and noodles. Stir until all are coated. Drop by spoonful on wax-paper-lined cookie sheet. Place in a cool room for several hours or overnight. Remove from wax paper and store in an airtight container in a cool cupboard or in the refrigerator.

Sherri's Macaroons

⅓ cup of flour
⅛ teaspoon of salt
2 ½ cups of coconut
1 teaspoon of vanilla
⅔ cup of sweetened condensed milk

Mix flour, coconut, and salt well. Pour in condensed milk and vanilla. Drop batter onto well-greased pans. Bake twelve to fifteen minutes at 350 degrees.

***

I was amazed to learn what delectable treats you can make with crackers. Here's a trio, made from Ritz crackers, soda crackers, and graham crackers. All of them are delicious, quick, and easy.

Kristine's Ritz Treats

Spread peanut butter between two Ritz crackers. Melt almond bark or white chocolate in double boiler or microwave. Dip crackers into melted chocolate. Place on wax paper or parchment paper. Decorate as desired before chocolate sets. Can be decorated for any holiday or occasion or just enjoyed plain.

Sweet and Salty

Cover cookie sheet with heavy-duty foil. Line with soda crackers.

  2 sticks (½ pound) of unsalted butter
  1 cup of brown sugar

Boil for five minutes. Pour over crackers. Place in four-hundred-degree oven for five minutes. Remove from oven and immediately spread one twelve-ounce package of semisweet chocolate chips over top. Top with walnuts. Freeze for five minutes. Break into *big* chunks.

Graham Cookies

2 cups of walnuts, chopped	1 cup of butter
1 cup of brown sugar	½ teaspoon of cinnamon

Grease jelly-roll pan. Line with graham crackers. Sprinkle with walnuts. Boil butter, sugar, and cinnamon for three minutes over medium heat without stirring. Pour over crackers. Bake in four-hundred-degree oven for six minutes. Cool in pan. Break into pieces while still warm.

***

I met my friend Elsie after Larry and I were married. Her husband and Larry's dad drove trucks for the same company, so she had known Larry since he was a young man. Elsie was one of our original "dirty dozen" and also worked with me in my Christmas party-plan company. We loved celebrating Saint Patrick's Day together. Every year for Christmas, she would make the most delicious butter horn rolls. She refused to share the recipe with me. Almost forty years lapsed, with me pestering her every year, before she finally broke down and gave me the much-coveted formula for her secret delicacies. It is with her permission that I share this recipe. For some reason, mine never taste quite as good as hers.

Elsie's Butter Horn Rolls

4 cups of flour	1 cake of yeast (can use dry yeast)
4 egg of yolks (save the whites)	1 teaspoon of vanilla
1 teaspoon of salt	1 ¼ cups of butter
1 cup of sour cream	

Sift flour and salt together. Add yeast and butter. Cut together as for pie crust. Blend in eggs and sour cream and vanilla. Shape into balls and divide into five balls. Chill.

Filling:	4 egg whites	1 cup of sugar
	1 ½ cups of finely chopped nuts	1 teaspoon of vanilla

Beat egg whites until stiff. Add sugar and beat well. Add vanilla; fold in the nuts.

Sprinkle work surface with powdered sugar. Roll each ball into a twelve-inch circle. Cut into twelve wedges. Spread each with filling. Roll from wide to narrow end. Bake at 375 degrees until lightly browned. Frost with thin frosting of powdered sugar, melted butter, and milk.

***

During the holiday season, we would occasionally go to a popular Italian restaurant in town for our company Christmas party. The matriarch of the family, who was then in her eighties, was well-known for the wonderful crème brûlée that she made daily. A friend of mine acquired the recipe from the lady's daughter and shared it with me. Every time I order this dessert in a restaurant, which I do often, I compare it to Mama's. I have yet to eat any that can even hold a candle to hers. Hope you will try this.

Mama's Crème Brûlée

1 pint of whipping cream	4 egg yolks
½ cup of granulated sugar	1 tablespoon of vanilla

Heat cream over low heat until bubbles form around edge of pan. Beat egg yolks and sugar together until thick, about three minutes. Gradually beat cream into egg yolks. Stir in vanilla and pour into six six-ounce custard cups or ramekins. Place cups in baking pan with half an inch of water in bottom. Bake in 350-degree oven until set, about forty-five minutes. Remove and chill. Sprinkle with two teaspoons of granulated sugar on each cup. Put under broiler until tops are brown. Chill before serving.

***

Larry and I had friends who invited us to attend a marriage-encounter weekend being sponsored by their church. Why not? It would be a nice relaxing getaway and sounded like a great means of enhancing our marriage.

The first day there, we got into a heated argument in the elevator. Just as I was using a few choice words to express my frustration, the elevator door opened, and there stood the priest who was hosting the affair, along with two of the guest speakers. I was mortified, wishing that I could just disappear. If the truth be known, they probably all chuckled on their ride down in the elevator.

The rest of the weekend was a nightmare. We were assigned to write love letters to each other, which was a good thing since we weren't speaking. By the closing ceremony on the last night, some of the love and joy had spilled over, and we had to admit that we were glad we hadn't left the first day.

The following month, we were invited to attend an encounter reunion. I was asked to take a cake. I made an angel food cake and decorated it from a picture I saw in a magazine. I frosted it with pink seven-minute fluffy frosting and decorated it with little silver sugar pearls and a red rose in the center. It was probably the most beautiful cake I have ever decorated.

It didn't make it to the reunion, however. When Larry arrived home and I so proudly showed it to him, he made a snide remark, and that cake somehow just slipped out of my hand, flew through the air, and landed all over the fireplace mantel and on his brand-new boots. I quickly disappeared into the bedroom, and not a word was spoken.

The next morning, he wanted to know if I was going to stop at the bakery and buy a cake to take to the event.

"Heck no, I'd rather tell the story and enjoy the reactions." I grinned with a gleam in my eye.

Everyone had a good laugh, and a lively conversation ensued about what an exciting, loving relationship we had.

"At least it's not a dull life," Larry added with a snort of dismissive laughter.

"Have you lost your marbles?" This was the question we were asked many times during the 1980s and '90s. In fact, Larry's license plate frame read, "I've lost my marbles . . . I'll buy yours." We became involved in buying and selling collectibles in the early 1980s and started doing antique shows in Washington and Oregon. When we began buying marbles, we had no idea that it would become our hobby and, for Larry, an obsession that led to a collection of a half million marbles. He amassed one of the largest collections of marbles in the state of Washington. He acquired marbles worth anything from a few pennies to hundreds of dollars apiece. He had antique marbles more than one hundred years old. His treasures included handmade Lutzes with swirls of cranberry, blue, and green and bands of finely ground copper that look like a Milky Way of gold dust. He had egg cartons full of expensive sulfide marbles with figurines suspended in molten glass, which had been imported from Germany in the 1800s. The pride of his collection were his Peltiers—multicolored marbles made in the 1920s and '30s with bold, eye-catching swirls. Like Tootles in the movie *Hook*, his marbles were his happy thoughts.

After attending several marble shows in the mid-West, Larry decided to start a club in the Seattle area, dedicated to the history, preservation, and collection of marbles. By 1994, the club was almost two hundred strong, and we were hosting four marble shows a year in Seattle, Santa Cruz, Denver, and Las Vegas. One of the highlights of our shows was our Marblerama, a marble-shooting tournament that we started in Seattle for the kids. It ended up being more fun for the adults.

The late Tom Snyder, host of the *Late, Late Show* in the 1990s, was in Seattle to tape his show from the Museum of Flight. He called to ask if he could come to our home to see Larry's collection. We had no idea that he intended to bring the whole crew and film part of the show from our living room. He invited Larry to be a guest on his show. We lived forty miles from Seattle and five miles out of the town of Monroe, up a quarter-of-a-mile dirt hill, and they sent a limousine to pick us up the night of the show. We were treated to a catered dinner at the flight museum. Larry was featured in several local newspaper articles and, in 2002, was the subject of an amazing story "Marble Mania" in the magazine *Antiques and Collecting*. His real claim to fame, however, is the cover of the April 1988 *Smithsonian* magazine—check it out.

Many of the people we met through our marble club became lifelong friends. Since most of my memories are associated with food, it is only right to include my dear marble friend Alan's best-of-the-best meat loaf recipe. This was his mom's recipe, handed down from his grandmother. Alan said it was usually a weekday meal because it was quick and lasted for a couple of days or could be used for sandwiches the day after being made. He has somewhat embellished it over the years (he says to make it healthier). He insists on fresh ground sirloin tip steak, hand selected. He also adds two cups of diced broccoli and mushrooms to the mix and stresses that the layering of the ingredients before baking is very important. Topping it with seasoned cracker crumbs adds a nice final touch of crust on the surface. Alan swears that people who hate meat loaf always request a second helping and the recipe after trying it.

***

Best-of-the-Best Meat Loaf

2 pounds of ground beef

1 ½ cups of bread crumbs

1 package of onion soup mix

2 eggs

¾ cup of ketchup (or chili sauce)

Mix thoroughly. Put into loaf pan. Sprinkle with Parmesan cheese. Cover with three strips of lean uncooked bacon. Pour eight ounces of herbal tomato sauce on top. Bake at 350 degrees for one hour. Serves six.

***

Alan's mother, Frances, was born in Brooklyn, New York, in 1926 and grew up in the Bronx. She was engaged to a guy who played baseball for the Brooklyn Dodgers when she met Alan's dad, Gordon, at a dance hall in 1946. I am so thankful that she ditched that ball player. Otherwise, I wouldn't have had Alan in my life. She was a delightful lady who worked her way up in the banking industry while raising two active boys. She and my mom hit it off right away when, at Alan's fortieth birthday party, they slipped outside to have a cigarette.

Another of Alan's winning recipes is this blue cheese dressing. I am presenting it in Alan's own words.

Blue Cheese Dressing

The blue cheese dressing is best if one uses a three-ounce brick or cube of blue cheese to break up or buy it already in pieces. Mash it with three tablespoons of lemon juice (I like fresh-squeezed lemons, but the ready mix is fine). Add five heaping tablespoons of real mayonnaise (the fat-free or low-fat kills it). Add just enough milk to loosen it up into a thick slurry. Place in the refrigerator overnight for best results.

Chapter 9

A new decade was quickly approaching, and as the twenty-first century drew near, I realized that my mother's saying "The older you get, the quicker time goes" now seemed to make sense. Larry was diagnosed with COPD (chronic obstructive pulmonary disease) and told that if he wanted to live a few more years, he should probably move to a desert climate. The dampness and mold in the Pacific Northwest were taking a toll on his lungs. I loved our home and was content with my job and at ease with the world; moving was not on the list of things that I wanted to do. Larry was eligible for retirement, and the company I worked for was willing to transfer me, so it looked like "Las Vegas, here we come." We had been going to Las Vegas every November for several years for the marble show and found it to be beneficial to Larry's breathing. It was the only time he slept without wheezing. In fact, I once woke up in the middle of the night, jumped out of bed, and turned the light on because I couldn't hear his raspy puffing and I thought he was dead.

The move went smoothly, and we were able to buy a house at a much-discounted price. We made an offer on it, and to our surprise, it was accepted. Only after the sale was final did I realize how much I did not like the house. It was in a nice neighborhood and close to the store where I would be working, but every day, I found something more that I disliked. We painted and had the bathroom remodeled. The washer and dryer were in the garage, and when the temperature was 114 degrees outside, it was at least 125 in that garage. I learned quickly to schedule my laundry any time after midnight.

As you came in the front door, there was a door to the immediate right where the kitchen was located. It was completely closed off from the rest of the house. Once you passed that door, you would never know there was a kitchen. The first year we were there, my brother and sister-in-law came from Seattle to visit. As he walked in the front door, he dropped his suitcase and quickly asked directions to the bathroom. When he came out, I proceeded to show them the house.

"Don't you have a kitchen?" he inquired with a perplexed look on his face.

When I look back now, I don't have many memories of cooking or trying new recipes or ever entertaining anyone. I simply could not, try as I may, learn to feel at home in that house. My only salvation was that I loved my job.

Las Vegas is a delightful place to visit or vacation, but living in a city where people drink and gamble twenty-four hours a day, seven days a week, and no one trusts anyone began to play on my sense of rationality. Working in retail, I watched people lie and steal and cheat every day. There was a shooting in the grocery store right next door to where I worked, which upset me tremendously. People were so unfriendly and rude. I tried to overlook the negativity and found myself becoming uneasy with my own options and choices. I was flustered by this less-than-ideal situation and second-guessing every decision I made. I was also missing my family and friends. When I finally woke up to the fact that I had three choices—accept it, change it, or leave—I quickly chose the latter. I was packed and out of there within a week. Larry pleaded with me to me to stay in Nevada, so while I looked for a place in northern Nevada, he sold the house. My only regret was that I had waited three years to make the move.

My sister had lived most of her adult life in Fallon and raised her children there. I was happy to be near family and closer to my kids in Washington. I was able to transfer again with the company I had been employed by in Washington and Las Vegas. Within the year, the company sold out, which gave me the opportunity to retire.

I found a house that was just being built in the town of Fernley, halfway between Reno and Fallon. Larry was pleased that I agreed to stay in Nevada, and I really liked the house. As I was driving from Fallon to Reno one day while the house was still under construction, I realized that I was going to have to find a restroom. Cruising down Main Street in Fernley, I spotted a friendly-looking little bar, the Silver Spur. My days of not walking into a bar alone were long past, and this looked much more inviting than the casino up the street. Walking into the place, I became overwhelmed with nostalgia. The rustic wooden rafters, the atmosphere, the people, and even the smell took me back to my loggers' bar in Washington. It was as if I had been transported back in time. I was introduced to the owner, Betty, who has owned the bar since 1982. She just happened to be looking for someone to tend bar two days a week. I was thrilled to be offered a part-time job close to home and excited to make new friends.

After fourteen years there, we laughed about the fact that she had never hired anyone "off the street" before that day. Betty and I became close friends, and she shared stories with me about her mother, Magda, who had come from Norway in 1929. Her dad worked for the railroad in the hot deserted Arizona town of Welton, just east of Yuma. Betty and I have often talked about how difficult it must have been, coming to a strange country, living in the desolate desert, and not knowing the language or anyone except her husband. Betty shared with me one of Magda's recipes, written in her own handwriting. I want to share it with you just as it was written.

***

Surkal (Norwegian Sour-Sweet Cabbage)

Cut one head of cabbage in fourths lengthwise. Take each fourth and slice thin lengthwise. Lay in a kettle one layer of cabbage, one tablespoon of flour, two tablespoons of caraway seeds, and a little salt—sprinkle this over cabbage. Dot with a few small pieces of butter. Repeat this until you figure out how much you want to cook. Pour water over till it is halfway covered. Cook until done, but do not overcook. Watch that it doesn't burn on the bottom. If water has cooked too low once it boils, turn it to low temperature. Keep covered at least until it is half cooked. When done, take off heat and season with vinegar and sugar to taste. The flour should thicken it so that it is not syrupy. But if it is not enough water when boiling, add some. It should be a little juicy. It doesn't take long to cook. You can cut the cabbage any way you want, but that was the correct way in Norway.

The seasoning: Start with a tablespoon of vinegar and three quarter teaspoons of sugar. Add more or less of each until you get the right sourness. Be sure to salt it like any other vegetable when cooking.

***

One of my first customers at the Silver Spur was a fellow from Montana. I have always loved meeting people from Montana and hearing their stories. The family of Keith's mother had moved to Montana from Maine in 1922. Her father was an engineer on the construction of the Fort Peck Dam. Three generations of his family worked on the dam. Learning that I loved to bake, Keith brought me a recipe in his mother's handwriting. It is titled "Cookies" but is baked in a nine-by-nine-inch cake pan. I have made this several times to serve at the bar. It is always a hit.

Poor Man's Cookies

1 cup of raisins	2 cups of water
½ cup of shortening	1 cup of sugar
2 cups of flour	1 teaspoon of cloves
1 teaspoon of cinnamon	1 teaspoon of allspice
½ teaspoon of salt	1 teaspoon of baking soda
1 egg	1 cup of nuts (optional)

Cook raisins in water until one cup of water remains. Combine remaining ingredients except egg and then add to raisins and water. Beat egg and add to mixture. Bake in nine-by-nine-inch greased pan at 375 degrees for twenty minutes. Dust with powdered sugar. Cool and cut in squares.

***

So many of the folks who came into the bar on the weekend mornings were not there to drink but to have coffee and visit, knowing that there would always be something good to eat. The bikers looked forward to my oatmeal cookies, and they all called me Mom. I loved it. The fellows liked to practice their pool games in the morning also. We jokingly pegged our Sunday morning get-togethers "early mass." One of my favorite customers (or "guests," as I prefer to call them), Sam, is from Leadville, Colorado, where my grandmother was born. His wife, Hannah, is from New York. She is a fabulous cook and would bring out-of-this-world desserts for special occasions. One of her exceptional dishes was made with fresh plums from their plum tree.

Zwetschgenkuchen (Plum Kuchen)

¼ cup of butter, softened
¾ cup of sugar
2 eggs
1 cup of all-purpose flour
1 teaspoon of baking powder
¼ cup of milk
1 teaspoon of grated lemon peel
2 cups of sliced fresh plums (about 4 medium)
½ cup of packed brown sugar
1 teaspoon of ground cinnamon

In a small bowl, cream butter and sugar until light and fluffy. Beat in eggs. Combine flour and baking powder; add to the creamed mixture alternately with milk, beating well after each addition. Add lemon peel. Pour into a greased ten-inch springform pan. Arrange plums on top; evenly press into batter. Sprinkle with brown sugar and cinnamon. Place pan on a baking sheet. Bake at 350 degrees for forty to fifty minutes or until toothpick inserted near the center comes out clean. Cool for ten minutes. Run a knife around edge of pan; remove sides. Cool on a wire rack. Yields ten to twelve servings.

Hannah's Cheesecake Bites

3 8 oz. packages of cream cheese, softened
1 ½ cups of white sugar
1 ½ teaspoons of vanilla extract
2 8 oz. cans of crescent roll dough
½ cup of melted butter
½ cup of white sugar
1 teaspoon of ground cinnamon
¼ cup of sliced almonds

Preheat oven to 350 degrees. Beat the cream cheese with one and a half cups of sugar and the vanilla extract in a bowl until smooth. Unroll the cans of crescent roll dough and use a rolling pin to shape each piece into nine-by-thirteen-inch rectangles. Press one piece into the bottom of a nine-by-thirteen-inch baking dish. Evenly spread the cream cheese mixture into the baking dish and then cover with the remaining piece of crescent dough. Drizzle the melted butter evenly over the top of the cheesecake. Stir the remaining half cup of sugar together with the cinnamon in a small bowl and sprinkle over the cheesecake, along with the almonds. Bake about forty-five minutes until the dough has puffed and turned golden brown. Cool completely in the pan before cutting into squares.

***

I was enjoying cooking again in my new kitchen and back to experimenting with new recipes. My husband likes to buy old cookbooks at flea markets, garage sales, and auctions. He brought home a stack of his new finds one day, and while thumbing through a 1932 edition of an old cookbook, I found an interesting recipe and decided to tweak it to my own liking. What a surprise when it turned out to be absolutely the best stuffed cabbage rolls I have ever eaten. I substituted V8 juice for the tomato sauce.

Stuffed Cabbage Rolls

1 medium head of cabbage
1 cup of cooked rice
1 ½ cups of chopped onion (divided)
¼ cup of ketchup
1 tablespoon of butter
2 tablespoons of Worcestershire sauce
¼ teaspoon of pepper
½ teaspoon of salt
1 pound of lean ground beef
¼ pound of Italian sausage
4 cloves of garlic
2 tablespoons of brown sugar
½ cup of V8 juice
2 cans (14½ oz.) of Italian-flavored stewed tomatoes

Cook cabbage in boiling water for ten minutes or until outer leaves are tender; rinse in cold water and drain.

Sauce: Sauté one cup onion in butter until tender. Add tomatoes, garlic, brown sugar, half a teaspoon of salt, and V8 juice. Simmer for fifteen minutes.

In a large bowl, combine rice, ketchup, Worcestershire sauce, pepper, half a cup of onions, and salt. Crumble beef and sausage over mixture and mix well.

Remove thick vein from cabbage leaves for easier rolling. Place half a cup of meat mixture on each leaf. Roll to completely enclose filling. Place seam down in a skillet. Top with sauce. Cover and cook over medium to low heat for one hour.

***

I was well pleased with this dish the first time I made it, and my husband seemed to enjoy it. As he swiped his napkin across his mouth, the inevitable question "What's for dessert?" rolled off his tongue.

"Nothing," I retorted without hesitation.

"How long does it take to make Jell-O?"

Oh boy, this was the beginning of what I labeled the "Great Jell-O War." I made up my mind that I would feed him so much Jell-O that the day would come when he would beg me to stop. I dug out my 1960s *Joys of Jell-O* cookbook, and the battle was on!

Believe me when I say there are more than 101 gelatin desserts—pastel dessert, mint julep delight, marshmallow parfait, raspberry Chantilly, and on and on. Why didn't I just serve him plain old green Jell-O every day and get it over with quickly? He was not about to holler, "Uncle!" and the challenge for me continued for at least two months. I was creating outlandish dishes, and he was loving it.

***

The good thing to come of my stubborn refusal to give up or give in was that I found so many tasty creations. One of the coolest, most flavorful pies I have ever made is a luscious pie that was created in the Florida Keys, where the limes grow big and juicy.

Key Lime Pie

1 package (3 oz.) of lime gelatin
1 cup of boiling water
2 teaspoons of grated lime rind
½ cup of lime juice
1 egg yolk
1 teaspoon of aromatic bitters
1 ⅓ cups (15 oz. can) of sweetened condensed milk
1 egg white
A few drops green food coloring (optional)
1 baked nine-inch pastry shell, cooled

Dissolve gelatin in boiling water. Add lime rind and juice. Beat egg yolk slightly; slowly add gelatin, stirring constantly. Add milk and bitters, stirring until blended. Chill until slightly thickened. Beat egg white until stiff peaks form and then fold into gelatin mixture. Add food coloring. Pour into pastry shell. Chill until firm. Garnish with whipped cream or whipped topping and lime slices if desired.

Jell-O is still one of Larry's favorite desserts, but he doesn't get it every day anymore. I finally surrendered, but the truce included a clause that I will keep that well-worn book close at hand.

***

My love for biscotti led to a long friendship with a couple from Portland, Oregon. Micki (her real name was Anna) and Chuck had done collectible shows for many years. He specialized in old watches and clocks. There wasn't a watch he couldn't repair. Chuck looked just like the pictures of Geppetto, the kind-hearted, humble woodcarver who created Pinocchio. His white mustache adorned an almost impish grin that seemed to draw people to him. It was not this glorious smile that intrigued me, however; it was the smell of freshly baked biscotti that beckoned me to their booth. Micki welcomed me with a warm smile, and before I could even respond, I had a piece of her heavenly biscotti in my hand. I don't quite remember if she offered it to me or if I just walked in and helped myself. For many years, we dealt in antiques with this inimitable couple. After Chuck passed away, Micki would visit us every year and always made biscotti bread for me.

Micki's Biscotti Bread

3 eggs, well beaten
1 cube of soft butter
1 teaspoon of anise flavoring
1 teaspoon of anise seeds
1 teaspoon of rum or brandy flavoring
1 teaspoon of vanilla
1 cup of sugar

Cream together and then add the following:

3 cups of flour
1 teaspoon of salt
3 heaping teaspoons of baking powder

Mix well. Divide in three sections. Shape each part into a long thin rectangle half an inch thick and bake on greased cookie sheet for twenty minutes at 325 degrees. Remove from sheet while still hot and slice. Coat with powdered sugar.

Micki liked to put it back in the oven after it was turned off and let it set. I might add that the aroma of this bread baking is mouthwatering.

***

Another of Micki's specialties was her bread pudding, which she made from a recipe she said she stole from a restaurant in New Orleans. I've never tasted better.

Bread Pudding

1 cup of sugar
¼ teaspoon of freshly grated nutmeg
½ teaspoon of cinnamon
A pinch of salt
6 eggs
1 ½ cups of heavy cream
1 tablespoon of vanilla
1 tablespoon of unsalted butter
6 cups of French bread (cut in one-inch cubes)

Butter a nine-by-nine-inch cake pan. Mix together sugar, cinnamon, nutmeg, and salt in a small bowl. Whisk eggs and add sugar mixture. Whisk in cream and vanilla. Add bread. Place in buttered pan and cover with foil. Bake in preheated 250-degree oven in a pan of water halfway up on baking pan for two hours. Remove foil and raise the oven temperature to three hundred degrees for about one hour or until golden brown.

***

Micki would make huge pots of delicious cabbage soup to keep in the freezer. She said it was for unexpected company. She was noted for feeding people who came to their home for watch repair or to pick up an antique purchase. You could always plan on eating whenever you visited. I have used this recipe often minus the kidney beans. It is good both ways and a very satisfying meal.

Cabbage Soup

1 pound of hamburger	1 large can (20 oz.) of tomatoes
1 large of onion	1 can (15 oz.) of tomato sauce
1 package of dry onion soup	1 teaspoon of salt
1 quart of water	½ teaspoon of pepper
½ cup of ketchup	1 tablespoon of chili powder
½ head of shredded cabbage	Kidney beans (canned or dry beans), cooked

Brown hamburger and drain fat. Chop onion and celery. Add other ingredients and simmer for two to three hours.

***

Bunco! What a fun dice game. I started playing Bunco in the early 1980s with a group of ladies whom I worked with in Washington. We played together for almost twenty years. We would get so rowdy and loud at times that I feared the neighbors might call the police. There were twelve of us, and we played once a month, each taking a turn hosting. We would snack halfway through the game on finger foods and have dessert at the end of the evening. In later years, my husband and I started a couples' Bunco night, and we would have a potluck dinner once a month.

When I moved to northern Nevada, my sister invited me to join her Bunco group. These were all older ladies and not quite as unruly as my original bunch, but the stories they could tell were more amusing than the game. My sister's dear friend Luella was the matriarch of the group, being at that time in her eighties. She is quite a character. She was a military wife and had lived in Germany for several years.

Whenever the round to roll sixes in Bunco came up, she would hoot, "Oh, my favorite number! I love sex." She was quick to explain to us that *sex* is the number six in German.

I use to sing the old song "Don't Bring Lulu" to her. She is a retired nurse and was always there to help my sister care for my mother in her later years. She loved my mother and called her Mutti, which is "Mommy" in German. At ninety-four years of age, she was still bowling and doing volunteer work at the naval base. Lu turned ninety-six in September 2017 and is still driving her 1974 Nova muscle car, Jezebel.

My sister use to say, "She drives that car like a bat out of hell!"

Lu's reply was "I have to drive fast with the windows rolled down in the summer because I don't have air-conditioning."

She loves to travel, going to the East Coast every year to visit family. I always felt like she was family to me and looked forward to going to Bunco at her house because of the most delicious treats she made.

Lu-Lu's Turtle Cake

1 box of German chocolate cake mix
1 14 oz. bag of caramels
1 small can (5 oz.) of evaporated milk
¾ cup of butter
1 cup of chocolate chips
2 cups of walnuts or pecans

In double boiler, melt caramels, butter, and milk. Stir until smooth. Prepare cake mix as directed on box. Pour half of the batter into a buttered nine-by-twelve-inch pan. Bake fifteen minutes in 350-degree oven. Take cake out of oven and pour caramel mixture over hot cake. Over the caramel, spread the nuts and chocolate chips. Pour and spread the remaining cake batter over all. Return to oven and bake twenty minutes longer or until done. Cool completely.

***

Another of Lu's sweet treats is a takeoff of a chocolate éclair and was my sister's favorite.

Sheet Éclairs

Bring to boil one cup of water and half a cup of butter. Add one cup of flour. Mix well. Remove from heat. Add four eggs, one at a time, mixing well after each. Spread on cookie sheet. Bake at 425 degrees for twenty to twenty-five minutes. Cool and flatten any bubbles. Mix one eight-ounce package of cream cheese with half a cup of milk. Add two packages of French vanilla instant pudding (four-serving size) and two cups of milk. Mix well; spread on cooled crust. Spread one eight-ounce container of whipped topping. Drizzle with chocolate syrup. When cool, cut into squares.

Chapter 10

"It can't possibly be fifty years!" I screeched as I opened my high-school reunion announcement. "Are you kidding? This must be a misprint."

I read it again, did a double take, shook my head, and, holding my hand up to ward off the truth, finally did the math in my head. "Yikes, it has been that long."

I hadn't missed a reunion, but until now, the years were nothing to cause this kind of panic. My mind wandered back to our last reunion, and I became overwhelmed with emotion, wondering who or how many would not be there. My anxiety quickly melted into anticipation as I made plans to attend.

It turned out to be the best reunion ever, at least for me. I had not stayed close to my schoolmates. I left home before our graduation and returned to visit only occasionally. It is amazing to me how one event can change the course of our lives. Reuniting with my old classmates and hearing about their life adventures made me realize that if there was anything we wanted to do, we should probably do it while we were still healthy and able-bodied. Larry and I had talked often about going south for the winters, becoming "snowbirds." When I returned home from the reunion, my eyes were glowing with excitement at the thought of this new venture. I wasn't sure how Larry would react to my idea, but with a pleased expression, he shrugged and said, "Well, I guess if we are ever going to do it, we'd better do it now."

One of my friends from the reunion had a fifth-wheel trailer, and he and his wife went to Yuma, Arizona, every summer, as do a lot of Montanans. His brother also had a place there, and we had several friends from Washington who either lived there year-round or spent the winters there.

We decided to make a trip to Yuma and check things out. I did not like the idea of buying and pulling a trailer, only to discover that it was not our cup of tea, so to speak. We ended up buying a little trailer that was set up on a concrete slab and skirted, obviously never meant to be moved. I don't know if it even had tires. We dubbed it the "dollhouse." It was completely furnished, down to the linens and silverware. Pots, pans, everything we would need came in the deal. It was in a lovely park with a swimming pool, a beautiful clubhouse, and lots of activities. We were now officially members of the Q-tip community—white hair and white sneakers.

We had a bountiful grapefruit tree in our yard, and our next-door neighbors, who were from Colorado, had a lemon tree. Everyone in the park shared their fruit—everyone, that is, but our next-door neighbors. I don't know what two people could possibly do with that many lemons—lots of lemonade, I guess. They would only pick them up to as high as they could reach and leave the ones on the top. They were both much shorter than Larry and our neighbor across the street. Every Sunday morning while the Coloradans were at church, Larry and the Canadian neighbor, Barbara, would raid the lemon tree. They would both have scratches on their arms, and I don't think they were fooling anyone as it was the neighborhood joke. Barbara gave me this fabulous lemon butter recipe that she would make with the fresh juicy lemons. It makes an amazing center filling for cake or is delicious for a fruit dip. Barbara served it in little pastry shells.

***

Lemon Butter

½ cup of butter   2 cups of white sugar
Juice of 3 lemons   5 eggs

Put all ingredients in top of double boiler. Bring to a boil and cook, stirring constantly until thickened. Put in pint-size canning jars. Let cool and then put lids on.

***

Another neighbor gave me a recipe for lemon squares, which were very much like the lemon bars that I had made in the past. They were a hit with everyone, and I couldn't make them fast enough. They would disappear after ten minutes out of the oven, so I would always make a double batch.

Lemon Squares

1 cup of flour	2 eggs
½ cup of butter	1 cup of granulated sugar
¼ cup of confectioners' sugar	½ teaspoon of baking powder
¼ teaspoon of salt	2 tablespoons of lemon juice

Blend flour, butter, and confectioners' sugar thoroughly. Press evenly in an eight-by-eight-by-two-inch square pan. Bake twenty minutes in 350-degree oven. Beat rest of ingredients together. Pour over crust and bake twenty to twenty-five minutes more. Do not overbake! (The filling puffs during baking but flattens when cooled.) Cut in squares when cool.

***

Making new friends and getting reacquainted with our friends from the past was indeed enjoyable. We didn't have much of a social circle at home, and in Yuma, it seemed that there was always a block party or a birthday or anniversary to celebrate. Everyone took turns hosting dinners. One of my friends from Butte—Bob and his wife, Chris— would have several couples over every year for Chinese dinner. Chris made all-authentic Asian food, and it was fabulous. Larry and I held a Mexican fiesta every year just before everyone left for the summer.

My Irish enchiladas were a hit. Our Bunco group met every month, and we all shared "finger foods." We did a lot of golfing, and I learned to play boccie. Oh, the good life!

There were several date farms in the area, and being a lover of dates, I had to scope out all of them. When I saw the sign that read Date Shakes, I thought that I must be reading it wrong or that it was a variety of dates. Oh no, it was, in fact, a milkshake made with dates. This was like finding the nectar of the gods to me! They make a paste of the dates by boiling them in water with a little sugar added and then blend it with vanilla ice cream and milk. I kept reminding myself as I indulged that dates are a very healthy fruit. Thinking that this had to be the best treat ever, we went to another date farm, and when Larry ordered an espresso, the lady inquired if he had ever had an espresso date shake. We have since even improved on it, making it with our friend Steve's homemade coffee ice cream instead of vanilla. You have got to try this absolutely scrumptious treat.

I always included my oatmeal dream-date bars as one of the desserts for our Mexican fiesta.

***

Oatmeal Dream-Date Bars

1 ¼ pounds of pitted dates, coarsely chopped
2 cups of orange juice
2 ½ cups of flour
½ teaspoon of salt (optional)
1 ½ cups of dark brown sugar, firmly packed
¾ pound of butter (3 sticks), chilled and cut into pieces
2 cups of old-fashioned oats, uncooked
1 ½ cups of shredded coconut, divided
1 cup of chopped nuts

Bring dates and orange juice to a boil. Reduce heat and simmer for fifteen to twenty minutes or until thickened, stirring occasionally. Remove from heat and cool slightly. Combine flour, sugar, and salt. Cut in butter until crumbly. Stir in oats, one cup of coconut, and nuts. Reserve four cups of oat mixture for topping. Press the remaining oat mixture evenly into an ungreased thirteen-by-eighteen-inch baking pan. Spread the date mixture evenly over the crust to within a quarter inch of the edges. Sprinkle with the reserved oat mixture. Sprinkle with half a cup of coconut, patting gently. Bake for thirty-five to forty minutes or until light golden brown in 350-degree oven. Cool completely in the pan on a wire rack. Cut into bars. Store tightly covered. Makes thirty-six bars.

***

Even people who claimed not to like dates would devour these bars and ask for more.

While in date mode, I happened to remember that my friend Ethel had given me two date recipes many, many years before. One was a candy that she always made at Christmastime, and the other was date pinwheel cookies. When we got home that season, I dug out these over-forty-year-old recipes and took them with me the following year when we went to Yuma. Dates are so plentiful there and much cheaper when you buy them from the farms. I could hardly wait to serve my guests my new old recipes.

Date Loaf Candy

3 cups of granulated sugar   1 12 oz. can of evaporated milk
2 cups of dates (pitted and chopped)   1 cup of chopped walnuts
1 ½ tablespoons of butter

Boil together sugar and milk until a drop forms a hard ball in cold water. (Test in cold water after cooking thirty minutes.) Add chopped dates and continue stirring until dates are soft and well mixed. Add butter and nuts and stir for a few minutes. Pour into buttered eight-by-eight-inch baking dish.

Date Pinwheels

½ cup of butter
1 cup of brown sugar
1 egg
½ teaspoon of vanilla

1 ¾ cups of flour
½ teaspoon of baking soda
¼ teaspoon of salt

Filling: ¾ pound (1 ½ cup) of pitted dates, chopped
¼ cup of sugar
⅓ cup of water

Cook until slightly thickened, stirring constantly. Remove from heat. Cool. Stir in half a cup of finely chopped nuts.

Divide dough in half. Roll each piece of dough on waxed paper into rectangle about eleven by seven inches and a quarter of an inch thick. Spread with filling. Roll tightly, beginning at wide side. Pinch edge to seal. Wrap each roll in waxed paper and chill several hours. Cut in quarter-inch slices. Place on slightly greased baking sheet. Bake at 350-degree oven for ten to twelve minutes or until lightly browned.

***

Another of our favorite things to do when we were in Yuma was to check out all the flea markets. I met a lady at one of the outdoor markets, and somehow the conversation turned to dates. She told me about a recipe she had for a date dip. It didn't sound too appealing to me, but I decided to give it a try. It is delicious!

Date Dip

1 cup of sour cream   ½ cup of mayonnaise

3 tablespoons of bacon bits   3 tablespoons of shredded cheddar cheese

1 ½ tablespoons of chopped green onions

1 ½ tablespoons of chopped celery   1 teaspoon of pepper

¼ cup of finely chopped dates

Mix all ingredients. Chill and serve with tortilla chips or fill celery sticks.

***

Our friends Ron and Shirley moved to Arizona several years before we started going there. Larry and Ron had worked together for twenty-eight years. When Ron retired, they built a beautiful home in Eastern Washington, but because of a rare skin disease, he could not tolerate the cold temperatures of the winters there, so they moved to Arizona. We visited them often, and they would come to Yuma to see us. Shirley was raised in the South and is one of the best cooks I know. She is also a gracious hostess; you never leave their home hungry. I'm sharing a recipe that she says she "just throws together" whenever she needs a quick dessert. It has come to be one of my favorites.

Pineapple Crunch Cake

2 cups of all-purpose flour

1 ½ cups of sugar

¼ cup of packed brown sugar

1 teaspoon of baking soda

½ teaspoon of salt

1 20 oz. can of crushed pineapple, undrained

1 cup of chopped nuts

In a large bowl, combine flour, sugar, brown sugar, baking soda, and salt. Stir in pineapple and walnuts. Pour into a greased thirteen-by-nine-inch baking pan. Bake at 350 degrees for thirty-five minutes or until a toothpick inserted near the center comes out clean. Let cake cool five minutes on a wire rack.

Icing:　⅔ cup of sugar　　　½ cup of butter
　　　　¼ cup of milk　　　　½ cup of flaked coconut (optional)

Combine sugar, butter, and milk in a small saucepan over medium-high heat. Bring to a boil; boil for two minutes. Pour over warm cake. Sprinkle with coconut if desired.

***

After eight seasons of going South, we decided that it was time for us to do some traveling, so we sold our trailer, a newer one that we had purchased, and sold our home and most of our worldly belongings. We purchased an 888-square-foot duplex with a detached single garage and a large covered carport. It has two bedrooms, one bath, and the cutest kitchen I have ever seen. We paved the front yard to make a cute courtyard and put wonderful raised garden beds in the back. We call it our "Farkle" house. For those of you who are not familiar with Farkle, it is a dice game. You have to have ones or fives to score, so twos, threes, fours, and sixes are "farkles," and you lose your turn. Larry is quick to explain to everyone that our house can entertain six, feed four, and sleep two.

"The guest room is circus-circus," he quips with a grin.

Downsizing was the smartest thing we have ever done. The house requires little upkeep, the utility bills are affordable, and we still have our garden every year and a peach/plum grafted tree, an apple tree, strawberries, blueberries, raspberries, and rhubarb. Oh yes, this is the good life!

We have traveled extensively, fulfilling most of our "bucket list." We have cruised the Caribbean, the Mexican Riviera, Alaska, and the Panama Canal. We drove most of Route 66, heading south after leaving Kansas City to revisit my past in Missouri and Oklahoma, continuing south to New Orleans, and taking a cruise from there to Belize. My greatest desire was to visit Ireland, but I always thought that I would have to do it alone as Larry stepped off a plane in Washington, D.C., in 2009 and told me that his feet would never leave the ground again. Thus began our train adventures. We have traveled almost every train route in the United States. Amtrak offers a thirty-day program that allows you to get off and on twelve times, so we have seen Florida and all the Southern Atlantic states. We enjoyed a few days in Savannah and went to Memphis to visit Graceland and spent a whole day at St. Jude's Children's Hospital. I got to see Churchill Downs even though it wasn't Kentucky Derby week. The train is a remarkable way to see our country—no stress driving, no worries about parking, just relax and take in the beautiful sights our country has to offer.

"How would you like to go to Ireland?"

"Am I hearing things? Did I hear him correctly?" I thought out loud.

He knew that this was my childhood dream, and he had often talked of seeing his ancestor's homeland, Holland. Now he is excitedly telling me about a thirty-eight-day cruise out of Boston, going to Bar Harbor, Maine (another of my bucket-list wishes), Nova Scotia, Newfoundland, Greenland, Iceland, Norway, Holland, Ireland, England, Scotland, and back.

"Are you out of your mind? We could never afford a trip like that. Besides, you won't fly to Boston to get on a ship."

"It is two years away, dear, and they are offering a 65 percent discount if you book now. We each have $200 sailing credits. Let's call and see if we can use that as a down payment and make payments on the balance."

I stared at him in disbelief, thinking, *Oh my god, he is serious.*

When I finally caught my breath and regained my balance, he explained to me that with the sailing date two years away, we had plenty of time to pay it off if we budgeted well. As for getting to Boston, we could take the train.

It is amazing how quickly two years passes and how easy it is to give up little things when you have a goal—no fancy coffee, no eating out, no bingo or shows, no gifts, no unnecessary purchases. It's not always easy to say, "I do *not* need those shoes."

Budgeting became a real challenge for Larry. By nature, he is a frugal man, being of Dutch and Prussian Jewish heritage. He has done the grocery shopping for the past fifteen years and faithfully shops the ads and clips coupons. What's the old joke about squeezing a penny? He was a meat cutter in his younger years, so he takes pride in buying beef and pork in bulk and grinding all our hamburger and making his own sausage. His sausage is better than anything you can buy in the store. Well, when he saw an ad for turkey at twenty-nine cents a pound, he hooted as if he had just won a jackpot. Off to the market he trotted with a wide grin and a faster-than-usual strut.

"They're not going to run out!" I bellowed as the door slammed behind him. "Oh my god, he will probably buy two or three at that price."

Six . . . six huge frozen turkeys! Our freezer was almost full. What on earth was he thinking?

He was so proud of his good buy that he handed one turkey to our mail carrier as she passed by. "Happy Thanksgiving, Martha," he chirped.

"Okay, I'll cook one this week. What about the other four?" I questioned.

He had that all figured out. "We need another freezer anyway, so eight meals per turkey at twenty-nine cents a pound. We'll just get another small freezer."

"We do not feed a family of eight," I argued.

He boiled a whole turkey, boned and strained it, and made sixteen quarts of turkey broth, which he divided in half and made soup—delicious soup, I might add. He made eight quarts of turkey noodle and eight quarts of turkey rice, and I made six turkey potpies. Looks like we really did need that new freezer.

***

Individual Turkey Potpies

3 cups of cooked turkey
1 can (10.5 oz.) of condensed cream-of-chicken soup
¾ cup of heavy cream or half-and-half
1 one-pound bag of frozen mixed vegetables, thawed, drained
Salt and pepper to taste

Mix ingredients and divide into six individual foil tins. Cover with pie crust or a biscuit mix topping and bake uncovered for thirty minutes or until crust is golden brown. Cool, wrap in foil, and freeze in individual freezer bags.

***

Hearing of my turkey dilemma, my friend and mentor Carol offered me a recipe for a turkey tetrazzini dish, which is not only tasty but also makes enough to add two extra meals to our freezer count.

Turkey Tetrazzini

2 tablespoons of butter
1 small onion, chopped
2 tablespoons of chopped fresh red bell pepper
1 can (10.5 oz.) of cream-of-mushroom soup
½ cup of water
½–1 cup of sharp cheddar cheese
2 tablespoons of sherry
1 cup of diced cooked turkey (more or less)
6–8 ounces of cooked drained spaghetti
1 tablespoon of chopped fresh parsley

In two tablespoons of butter, sauté onion and red bell pepper until tender. Add soup, water, cheese, and sherry and cook over low heat until cheese is melted, stirring often. Stir in turkey, spaghetti, and fresh parsley. Cover and cook at 350 degrees for half an hour (more or less). Garnish with a bit of pimento and parsley if desired. Enjoy!

***

It may have taken us two years of scrimping, but we made it! The time went quickly as we both stayed busy. I spent my time making lists, reserving hotels, planning schedules, and asking questions. We could hardly think or talk about anything else. We finally boarded the train, overthinking every detail of the trip. We were eager to get on the ship and let our cares flow away for thirty-eight days.

"I will not order naked!"

My husband is not a soft-spoken man, so his voice resounded across the entire lido deck of the ship, where the guests were enjoying their leisure lunch. Heads turned, and there were a few muffled gasps and giggles. I quickly explained to him that if he wanted his french fries without seasoned salt or cheese and chili, he was going to have to order them the way they were listed on the reader board—"naked."

We now had the attention of several dozen people, a few of whom were laughing. This was just the beginning of what turned out to be my quest to make old cranky people who seemed to have no joy in their lives smile or, better yet, laugh out loud.

Whenever I watch musical movies, I have to wonder who really breaks out in song and dance in an everyday normal setting. I always wanted to do it, and I finally got my chance one morning on the ship when I smiled at a crotchety old fart in a wheelchair. He mumbled something gruffly and made a god-awful face.

Without hesitation and not giving it any thought, I bent down to his level and started to sing, "It isn't any trouble just to s-m-i-l-e."

I sang the whole song, and to my surprise and delight, some of the onlookers began clapping, tapping their feet, and singing along. With his face now upturned to me and swaying to the tune, he held his arms out as if to hug the world. He began to smile and was engaging in conversation with some of the other folks. I walked away lighthearted with a huge smile on my face.

On a ship with almost two thousand people, you rarely see the same faces on a daily basis. The last day of the cruise, we were on the elevator, and when it stopped and the door opened, a man inquired, "Are you going up?"

I began singing, "Up, up, and away," and I heard a voice coming from the back of the elevator.

"Oh my gosh, she is still singing."

I was waiting for the elevator early one morning, and when one finally stopped, I politely inquired if it was going up.

"Read the light," the not-so-friendly gentleman snapped at me.

Before the door closed completely, I pushed the button again. The door opened. Oh my, if looks could kill. I hadn't done it intentionally.

"Lay off that damn button," he growled, pulling down his glasses and looking scornfully at me over the rims.

"I am so sorry, sir, are you going down?" I didn't mean it to be funny; the words just slipped out of my mouth as the door began to close again.

Before he could answer, as the door was closing, someone else walked up and pushed the Up button. By now, this guy was hot and really thought that I was messing with him.

"I hope I never see him again," I mumbled when the door finally closed.

Everyone who had gathered to wait for the elevator began giggling, making faces, and winking at one another.

The very next day, as I was strolling the deck, I see this fellow walking with a group of people toward me. I couldn't decide whether to turn around and walk the other way or just pass him by and act like I didn't recognize him. Before I could make my move, he approached me and tapped me on the shoulder. I felt my insides quivering as I avoided making eye contact with him. I do not deal well with confrontation.

"You know, lady, you made my day yesterday. I had to chuckle at the look on your face as the elevator door finally closed. I was hoping I'd run into you again."

He was repeating the whole scenario to his comrades, with his eyes wide and a huge belly laugh, which had them all dissolving into laughter. What could I do but laugh with them?

One evening we were eating at the buffet, and when I saw the dessert selection, I couldn't decide if I wanted carrot cake or cherry cheesecake. I hesitantly put one of each on my plate. A very dignified gentleman standing next to me glanced disapprovingly at me.

I took a deep breath, smiled at him, and coyly uttered, "I'm a recovering anorexic, and this is my reward."

He raised his eyebrows, gave me a look that radiated superiority, turned his back, and walked away. I couldn't keep a straight face.

Another evening in the dining room, a very slender, stylish lady at the table next to us refused dessert. I reminded her using a very quiet voice of all the people on the *Titanic* who refused dessert on that cold April night. Guess who ordered cheesecake before me the next day.

"You are right, my dear." She smiled sweetly at me. "Life is too short to deprive oneself."

My crusade to make people smile or laugh, even just for a day, was, in my mind, a success, even at the cost of making a fool of myself. I will cherish the memories, not only of the phenomenal places we visited but also of all the awesome people we met and new friends we made along the way. We now have invitations to visit people in Georgia, South Carolina, Arizona, California, and New York.

You might think that thirty-eight days on a ship would get a little humdrum, but with all the fabulous food and nightly entertainment, the ports of call every few days, and the excursions, there is never a dull or boring moment. Afternoons would find us out on the deck playing dominos or dice games.

We became acquainted with a delightful couple from Georgia who sat at the table next to us. They played cribbage. I don't play cards, but cribbage is Larry's game of choice, so when he and Bill were engaged in a hot card game, Ingrid and I would discuss—what else?—food.

Ingrid was born in Berlin in 1940 and married her first husband, who was in the U.S. Army, there in 1958. She came to the United States in 1960 and became a citizen in 1963. Her husband was killed in Vietnam in 1966. She credits her cooking skills and her ability to adapt any recipe to taste to her grandmother, Olga, who was born in Koswalk/Pommern (somewhere between Germany and Poland) in 1888. I could almost taste the red cabbage of Ingrid's grandmother as she described it to me, and I was thrilled when she sent me the recipe.

***

Red Cabbage

1 large, very firm red cabbage (usually better after a frost has hit it)
1 medium apple—peeled, cored, and chopped
1 small onion, chopped
Salt to taste
Peppercorns (or black pepper)
12 whole cloves (or ½–1 teaspoon of powdered cloves)
¼ cup of butter (or 1 tablespoon of bacon drippings)

Shred cabbage (like slaw). Add all other ingredients. Add enough water to cook. Cook twenty to thirty minutes on medium heat. If water cooks down, add a little at a time. When cabbage has cooked to desired tenderness, add white cider vinegar and sugar to taste. You may add more salt, pepper, cloves, vinegar, and sugar until you get the taste that pleases you most.

This recipe has no exact measurements. Use the "pinch and taste" method. If cabbage has too much liquid, spoon some out or make a slurry of a little water and flour and thicken the cabbage slightly.

Ingrid's note: "This gets better the more times you warm it up."

***

Another of Olga's recipes that Ingrid fondly remembered was her potato pancakes. She smiled, telling me about her and her brother taking turns eating them fresh out of the frying pan as fast as Grandma could make them.

Potato Pancakes

2 large potatoes, grated (you can use the food processor)
2 eggs
Salt to taste
Enough flour to bind mixture (not too much)
Oil to fry

Mix grated potatoes, salt, and eggs. If potatoes are watery, add some more flour. Fry.

Ingrid's notes: "If you use old potatoes, cakes may come out gray. Always use nice firm white potatoes. You can also add chopped onion, garlic, or whatever turns you on to the mix. Can be served as a side dish or alone with syrup."

***

Ingrid remarried, and her husband was transferred to Prum Post, Germany, in 1971. There, she met Frau Schmidt, a German lady who shared meals with them (American style) and was not afraid to let her know if the food was good or not. This next recipe comes from Frau Schmidt, translated from German.

Naunzen (Mardi Gras) Cookies

½ cup of sugar
4 tablespoons of butter
Pinch of salt
4 eggs

4 ounces of rum

3 ounces of rosewater (can substitute water)

1 teaspoon of vanilla

Beat everything together until bubbly. Add enough flour to make a fairly firm dough (no exact measurement available). Dough will be elastic. Roll out very thin on floured board. Cut into strips and deep-fry (like doughnuts). Dust with powdered sugar.

***

Another favorite cookie recipe came from Ingrid's sister-in-law in the 1960s.

Cornflake Cookies

1 cup of butter	1 cup of oil
1 cup of white sugar	1 cup of brown sugar
1 egg	1 teaspoon of vanilla
3 ½ cups of sifted flour	1 teaspoon of salt
1 teaspoon of baking soda	2 cups of cornflakes (crushed)
1 cup of uncooked oatmeal	1 cup of chopped pecans

Mix butter, oil, sugars, egg, and vanilla. Add flour, salt, and soda. Stir in cornflake crumbs, oatmeal, and pecans. Mix well. Drop by teaspoonful on lightly greased (or sprayed) cookie sheet. Bake at 350 degrees for ten to fifteen minutes or until brown. Makes eight to ten dozen cookies.

***

I wasn't aware that Georgia is the "fruitcake capital" of the world. For people who do not like the traditional fruitcake, Ingrid offers this great alternative.

Fruitcake Cookies

1 cup of brown sugar
4 eggs, well beaten
3 cups of flour
½ teaspoon of nutmeg
1 teaspoon of vanilla
½ cup of butter
1 teaspoon of baking soda
3 tablespoons of buttermilk
½ cup of whiskey
1 pound of white raisins
1 cup of black walnuts
2 cups of chopped pecans
½ pound of candied cherries, chopped
1 pound of glazed pineapple, chopped

Take half a cup of flour out and roll fruit and nuts in it. Beat sugar, butter, and eggs well. Add sifted flour with soda and nutmeg. Add fruit and nuts and mix well. Add milk, whiskey, and vanilla. Chill batter overnight. Drop by teaspoonful on greased cookie sheet. Bake at 350 degrees until brown, about twenty minutes. Makes about one hundred cookies.

***

The people I have met over the past sixty years and the amazing food that they have shared with me has always been something that I wanted to pass on. So here it is—well, some of it.

What prompted me to finally put it in writing was a phone call that I received from my granddaughter Michelle one day.

"Grandma, I need your Mississippi mud recipe." Her voice sounded almost frantic.

"Okay, honey, I'll e-mail it to you."

"No, no, I need it right now" came her anxious reply.

As I was looking for it, I began to tell her about my dear friend Evelyn who had given me the recipe many, many years ago.

"You know, Grandma, you should really write a book. You have a story to go with every recipe you have."

So many stories. Looking back and thinking about all the people who have touched my life and reliving special moments with every tattered recipe card, scrap of paper, bar coaster, and anything I could find to write on has brought me so much joy, along with a few tears.

My hope is that my family and friends and everyone who reads my stories will try some of these amazing recipes and know that my heart and love is instilled in every word.

Index